# SUPER CUTE FAIRIES & MERMAIDS

## Fantasy Coloring Book

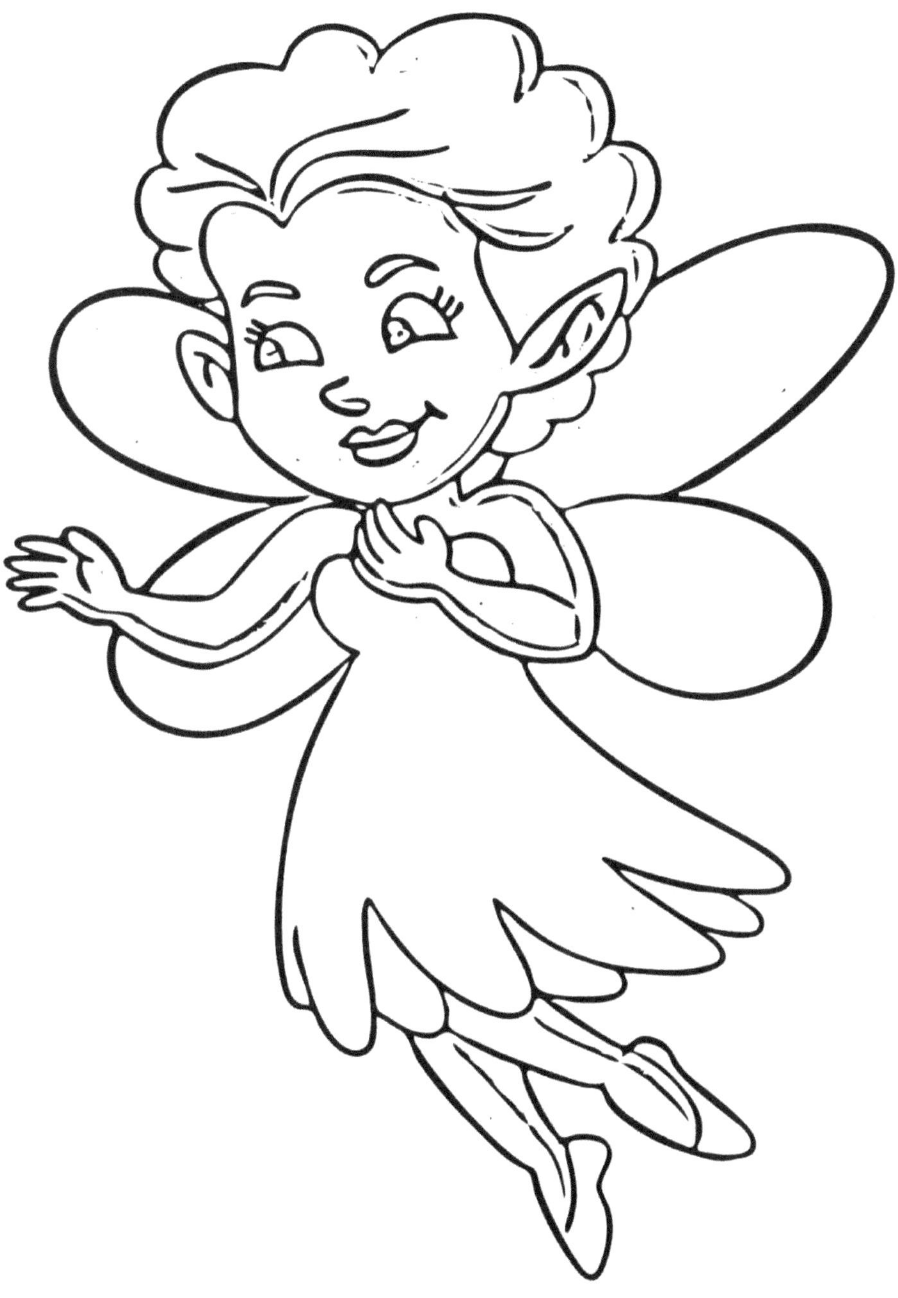

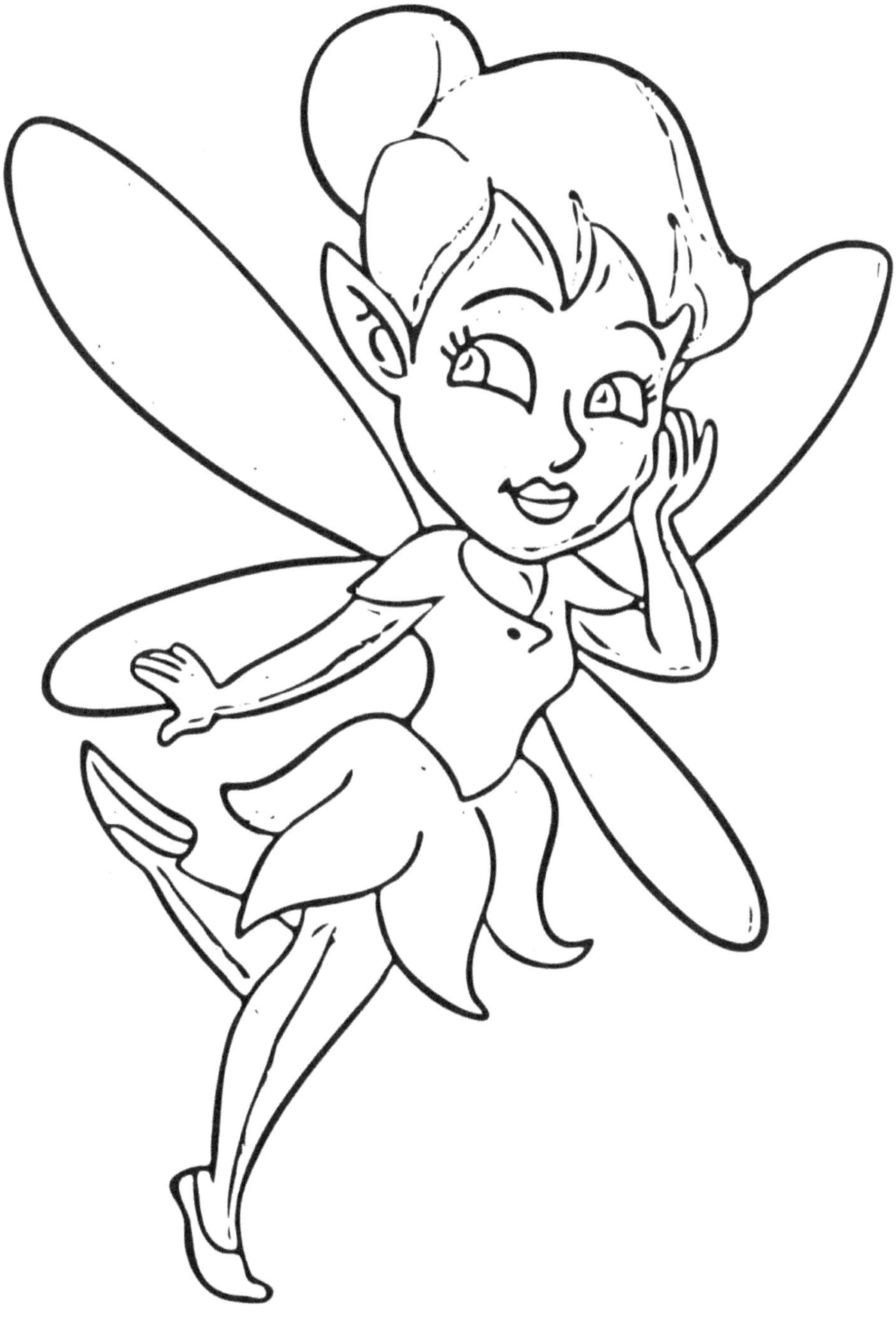

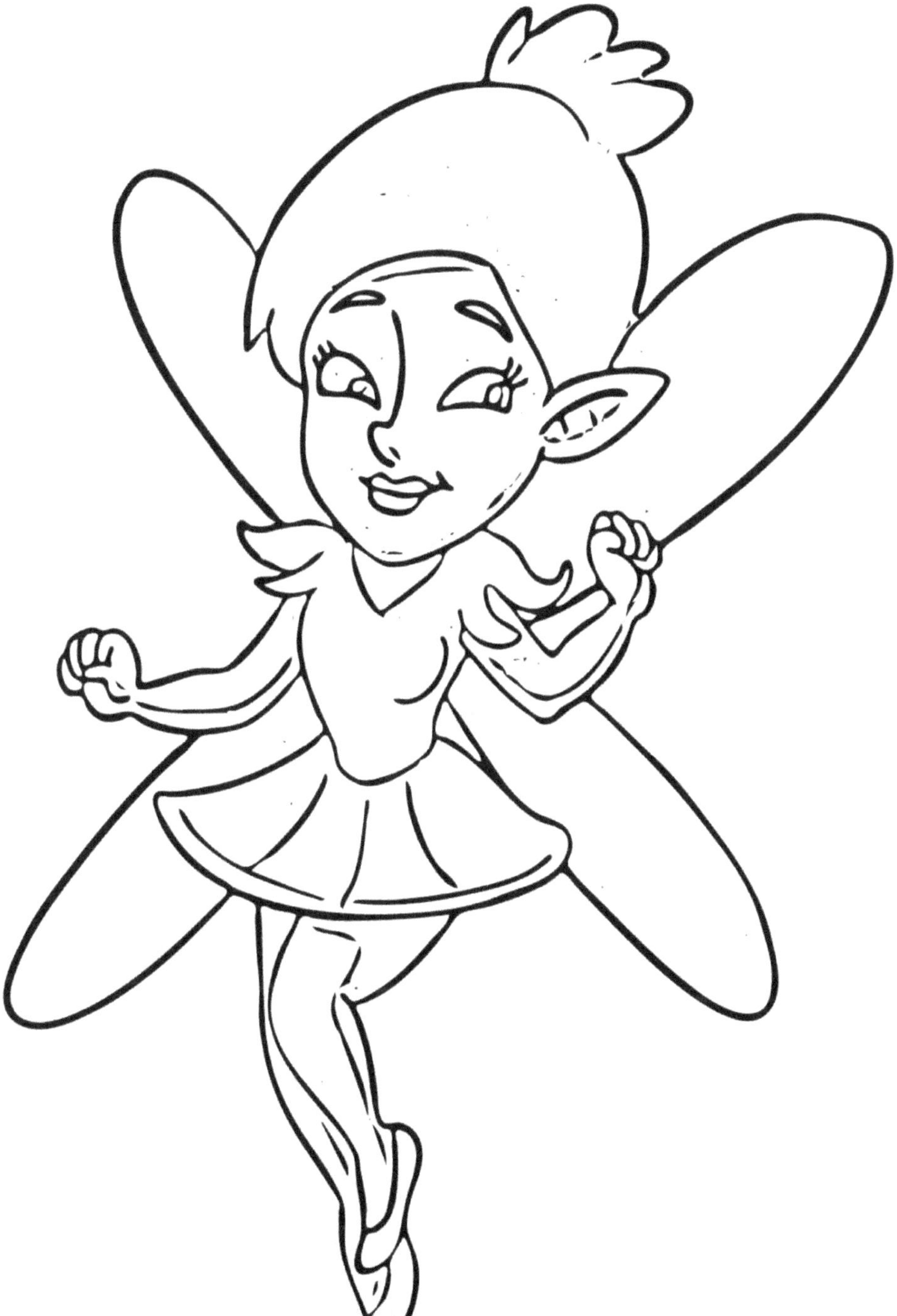

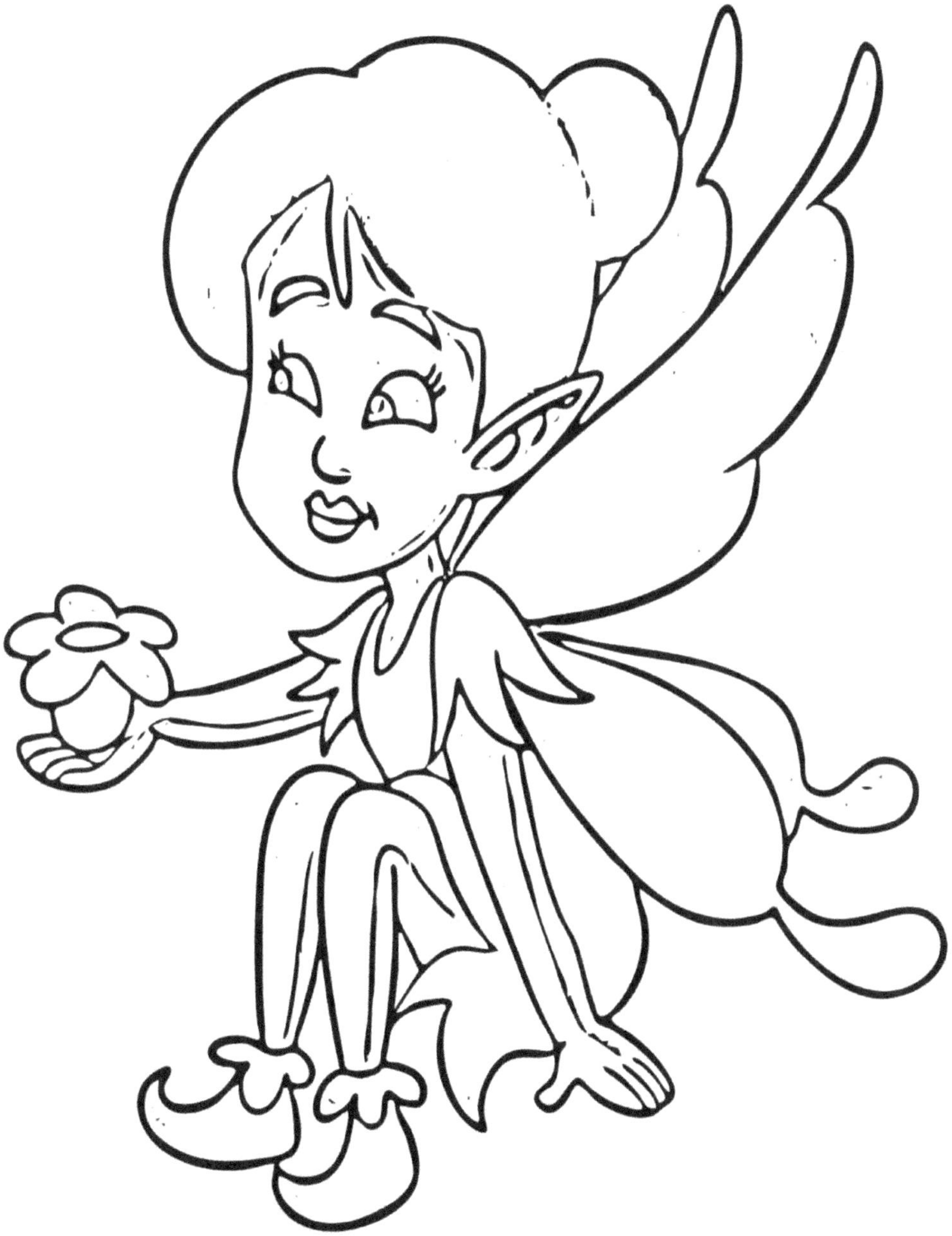

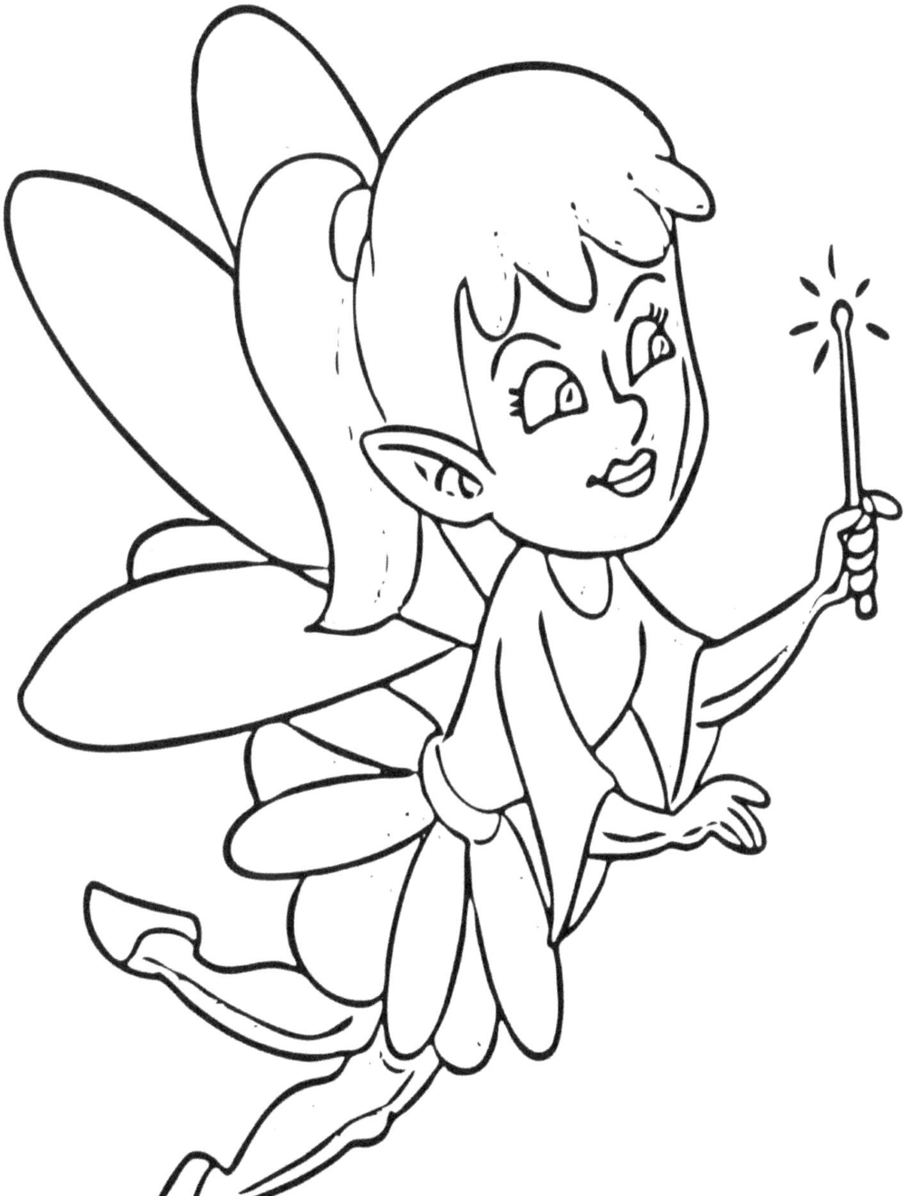

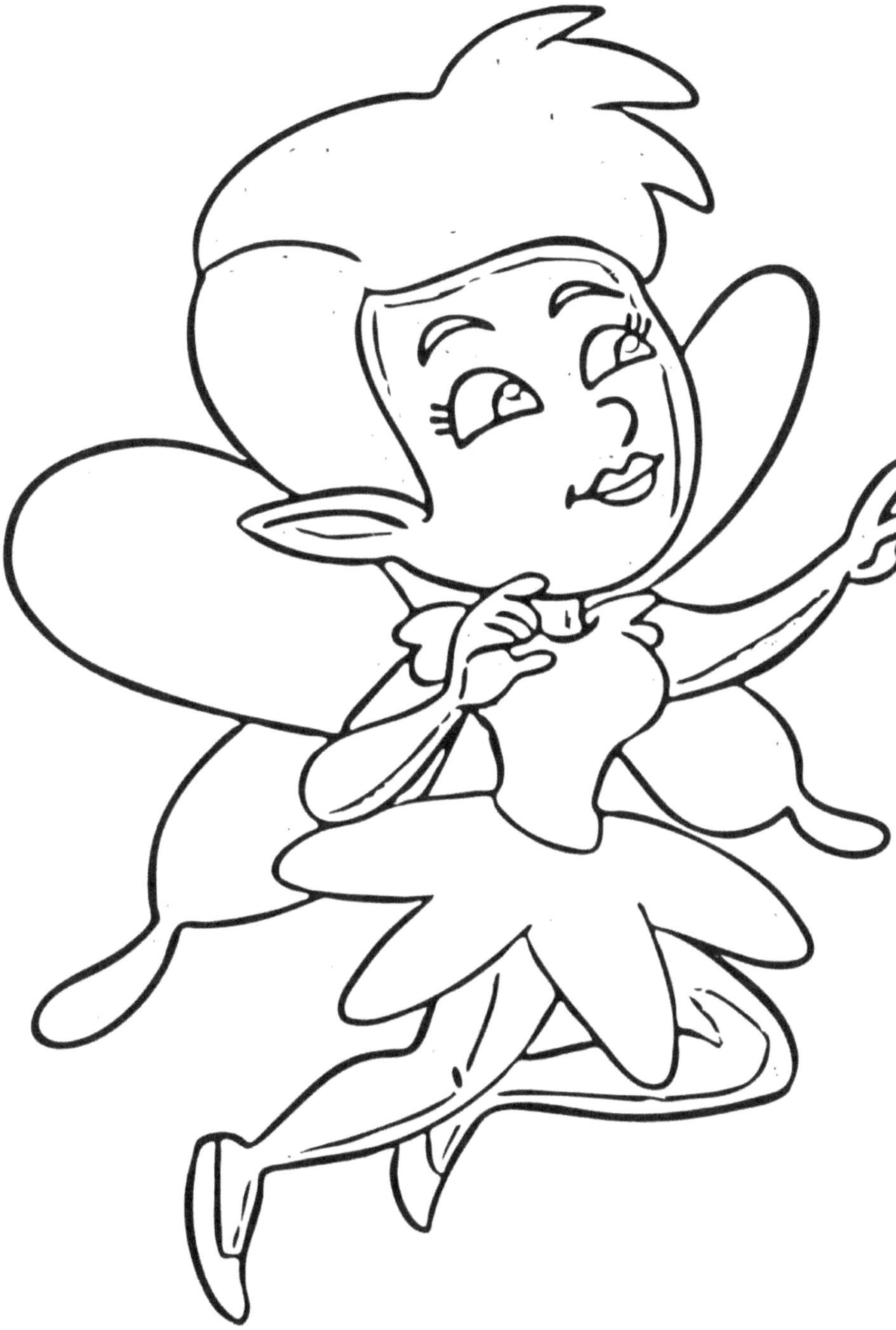

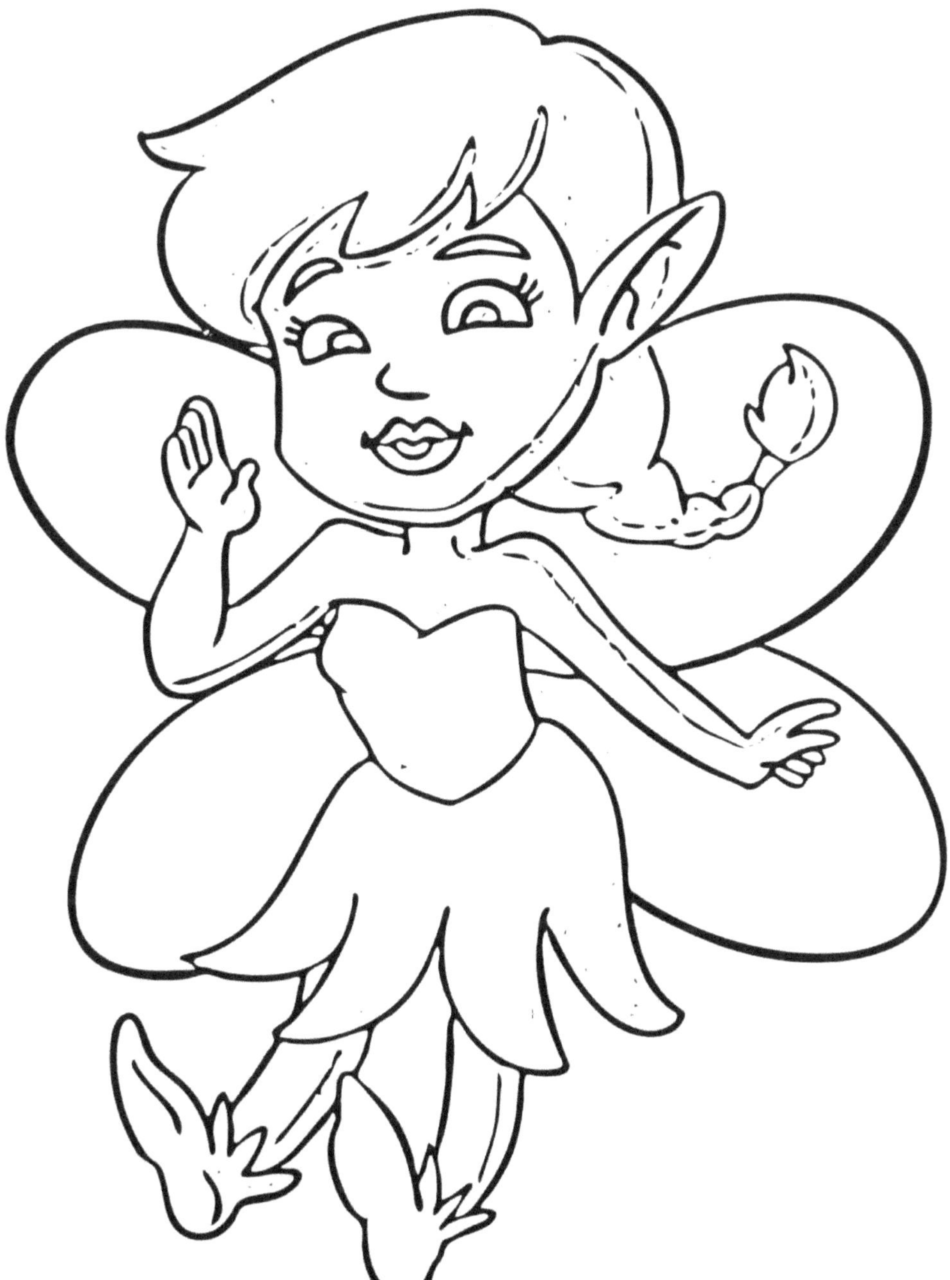

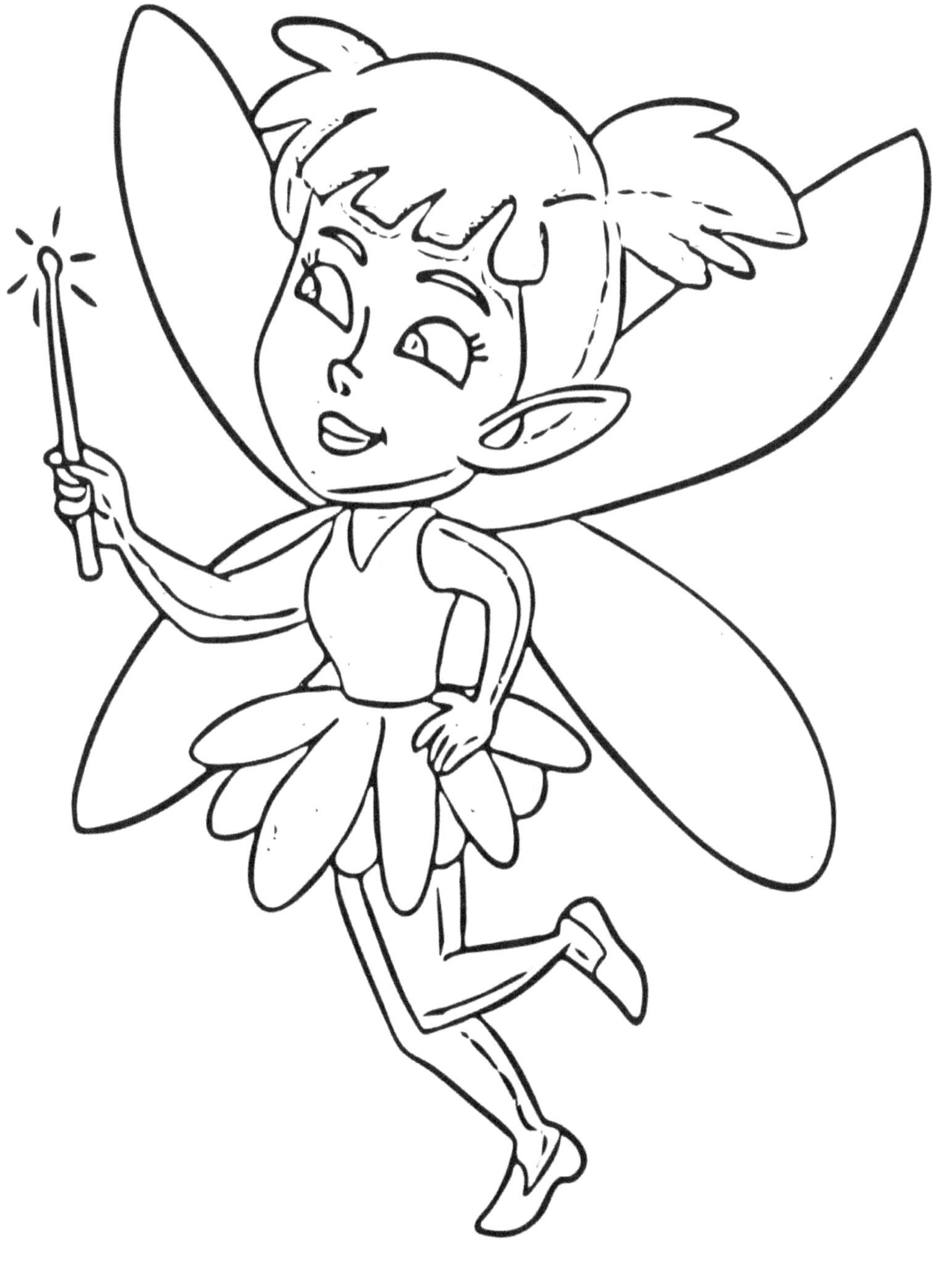

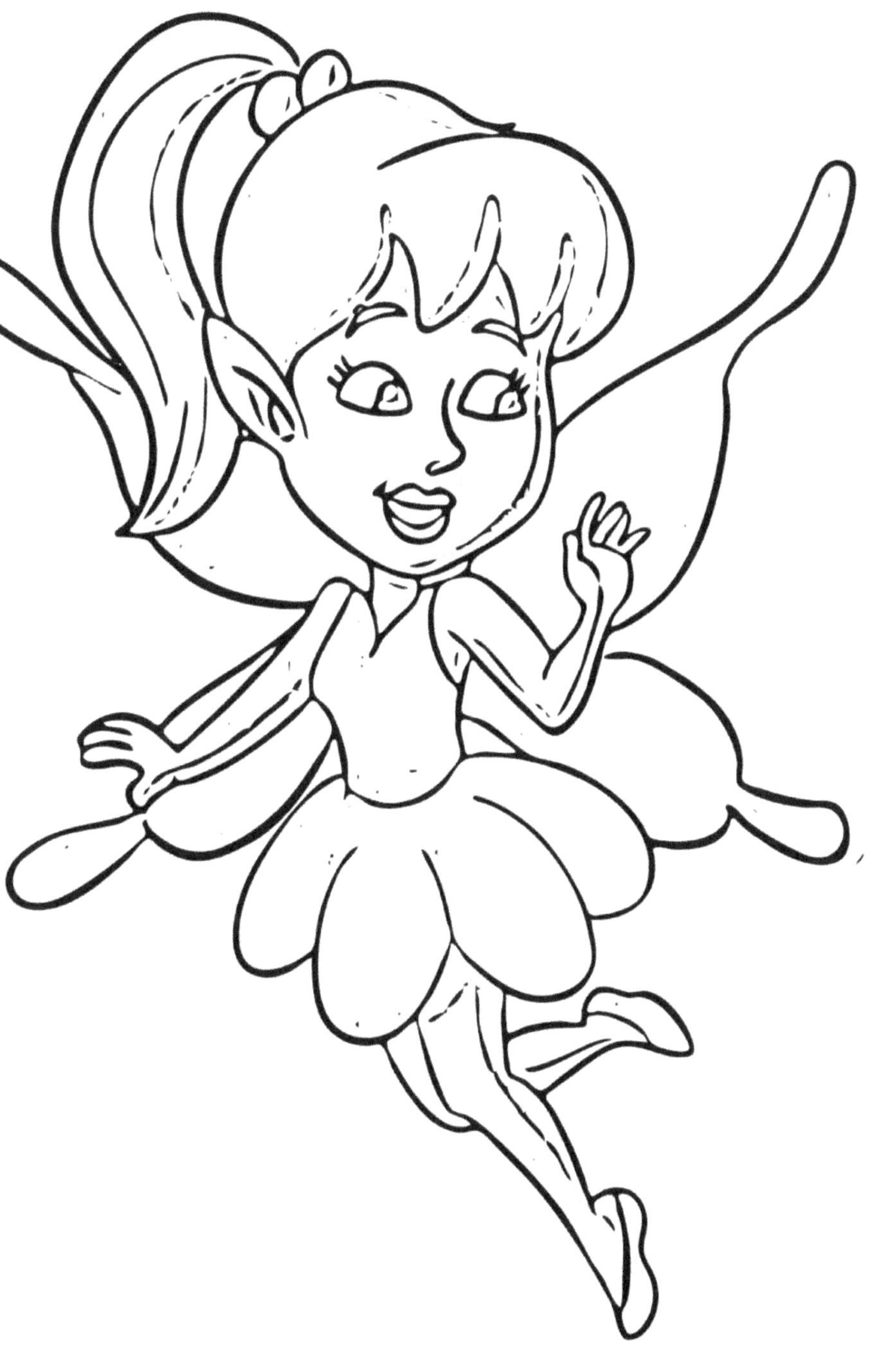

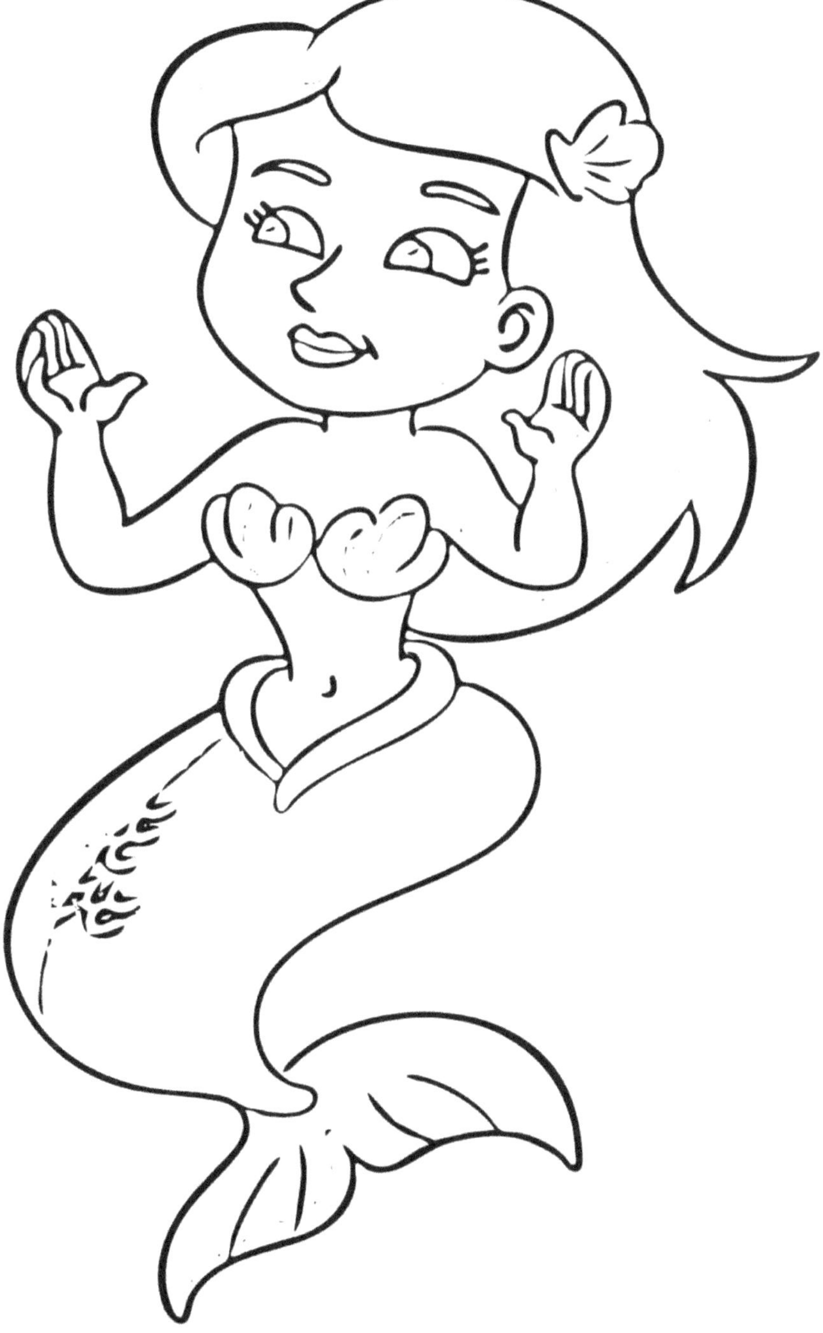

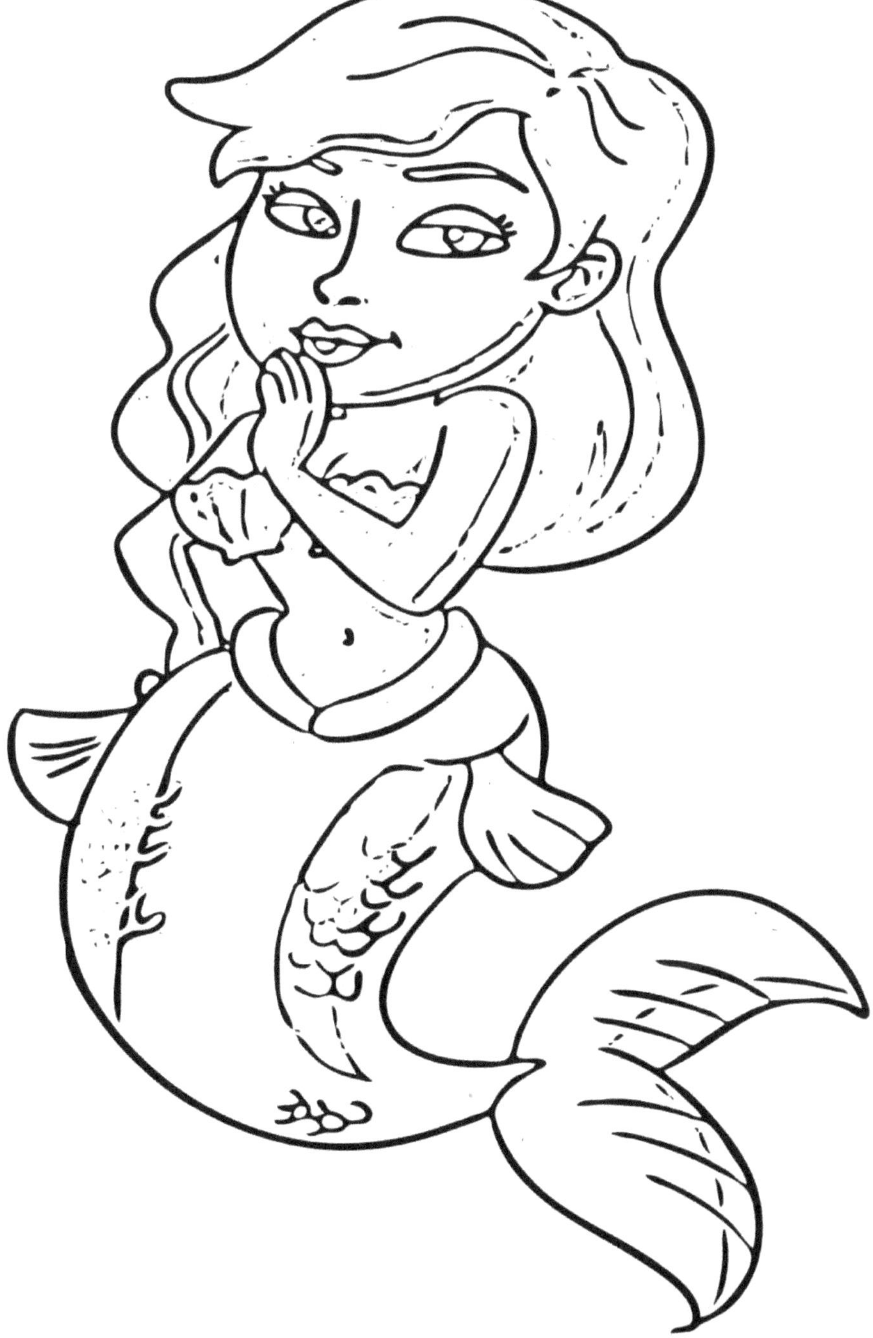

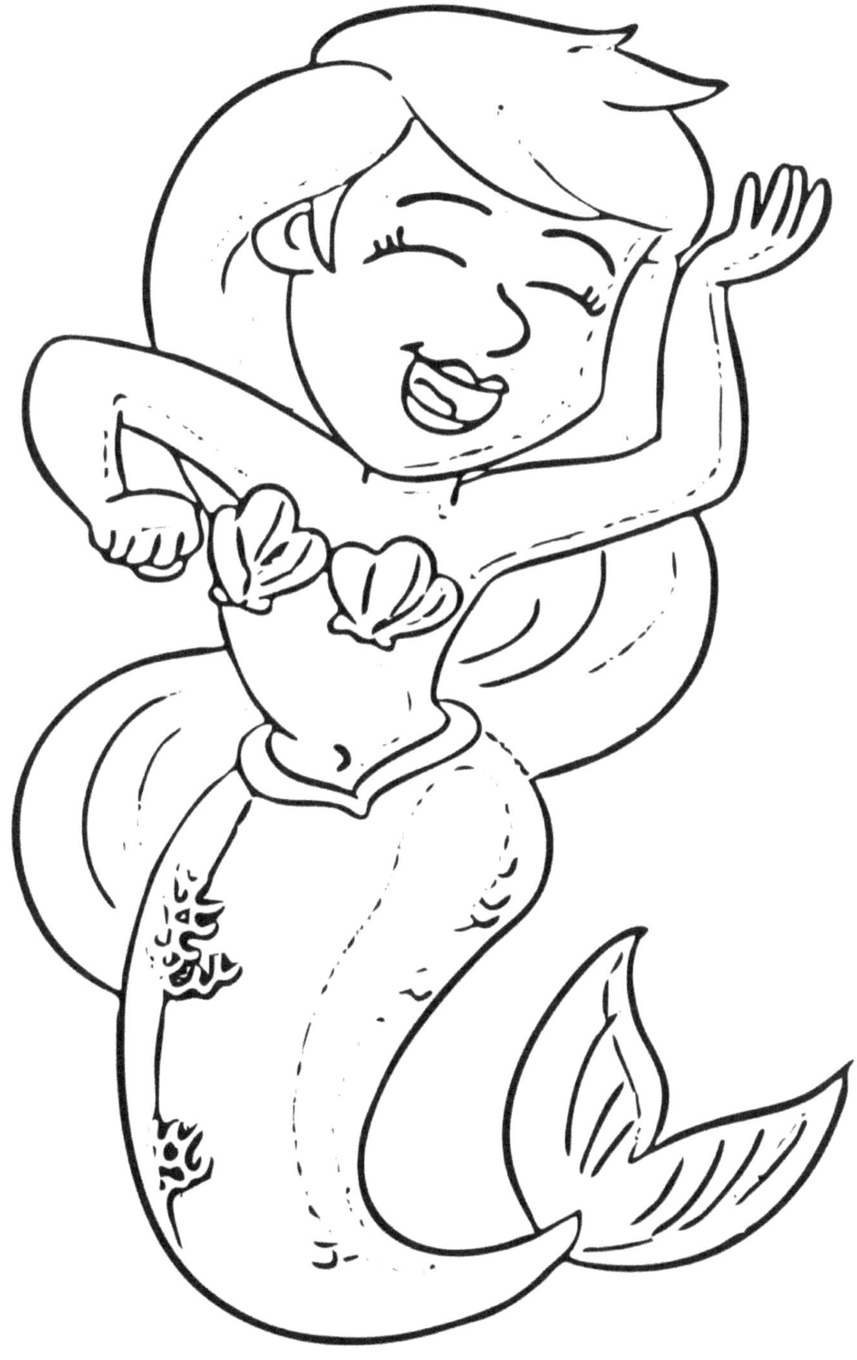

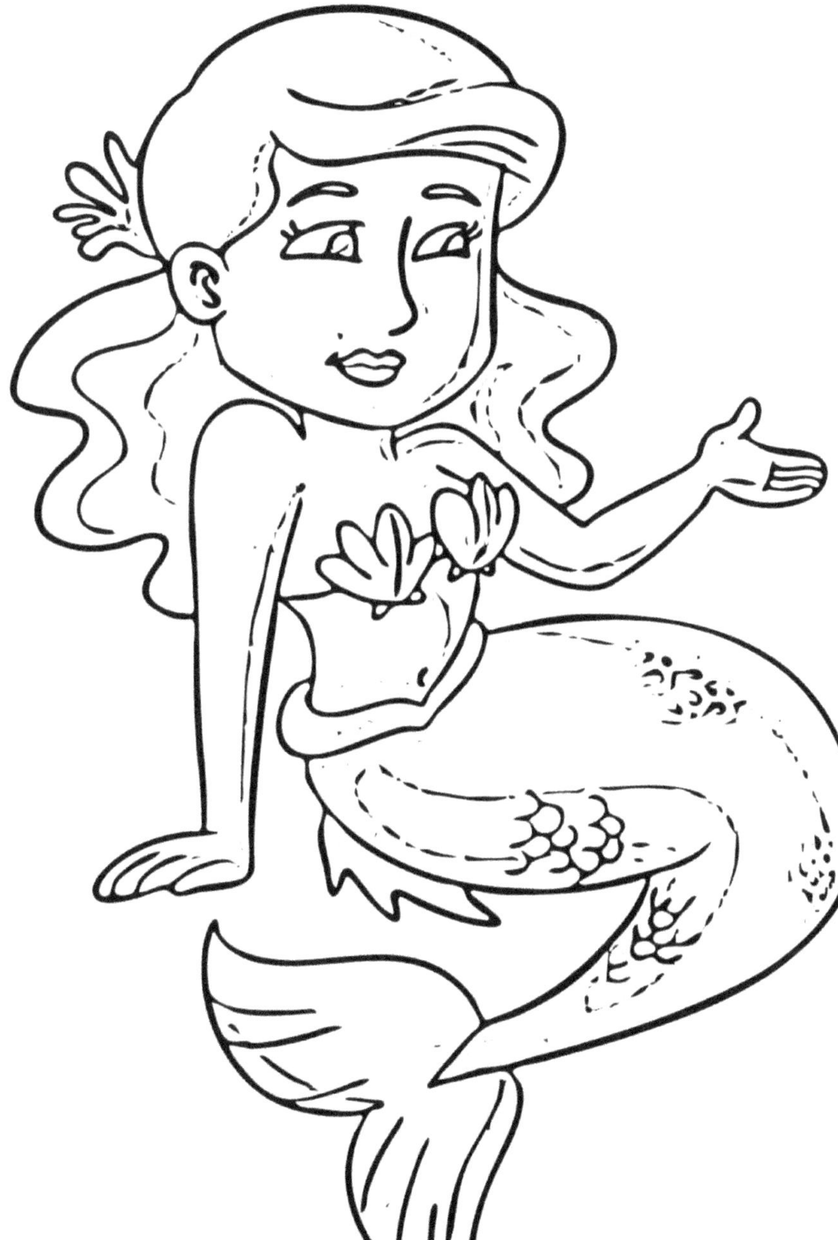

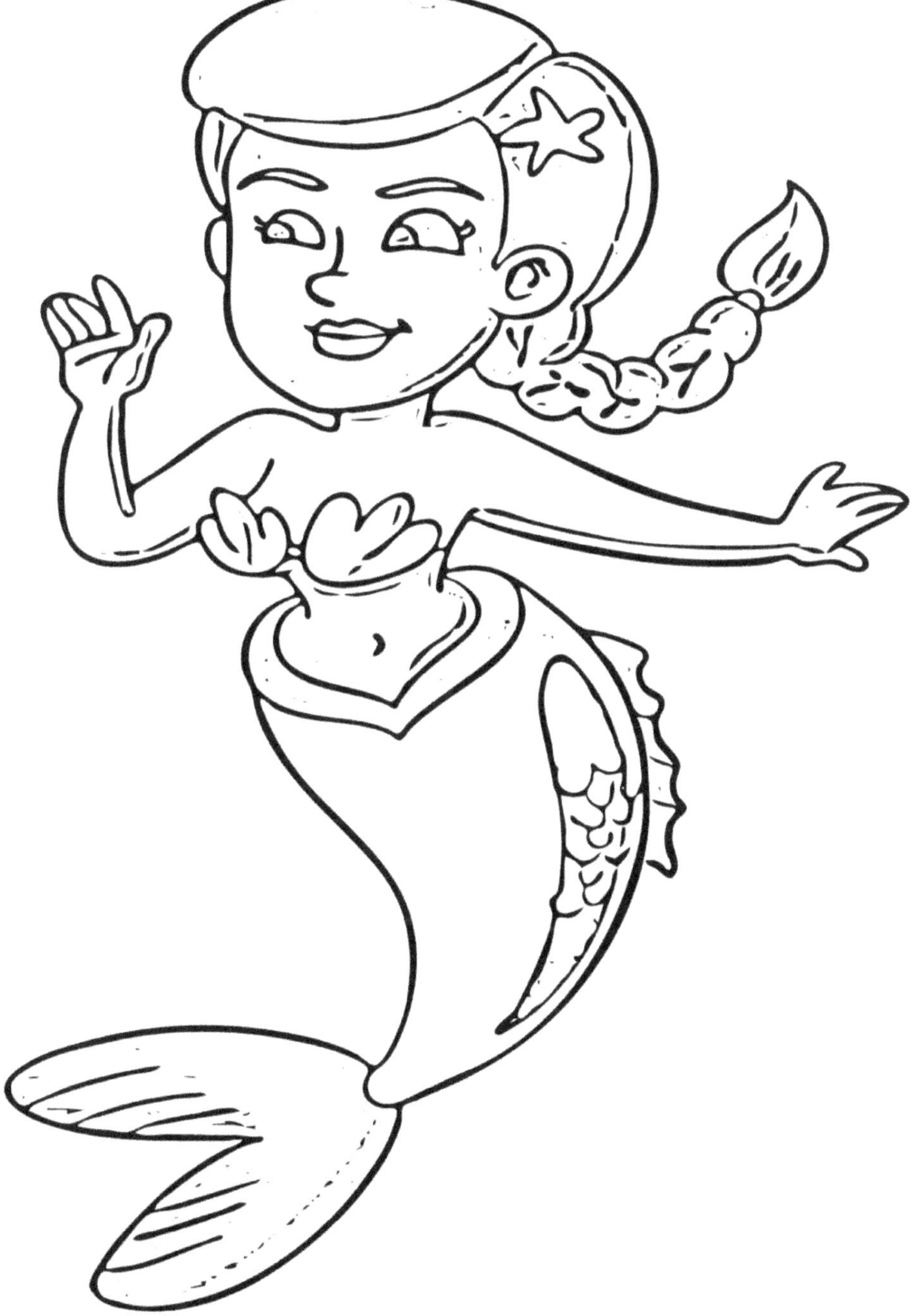

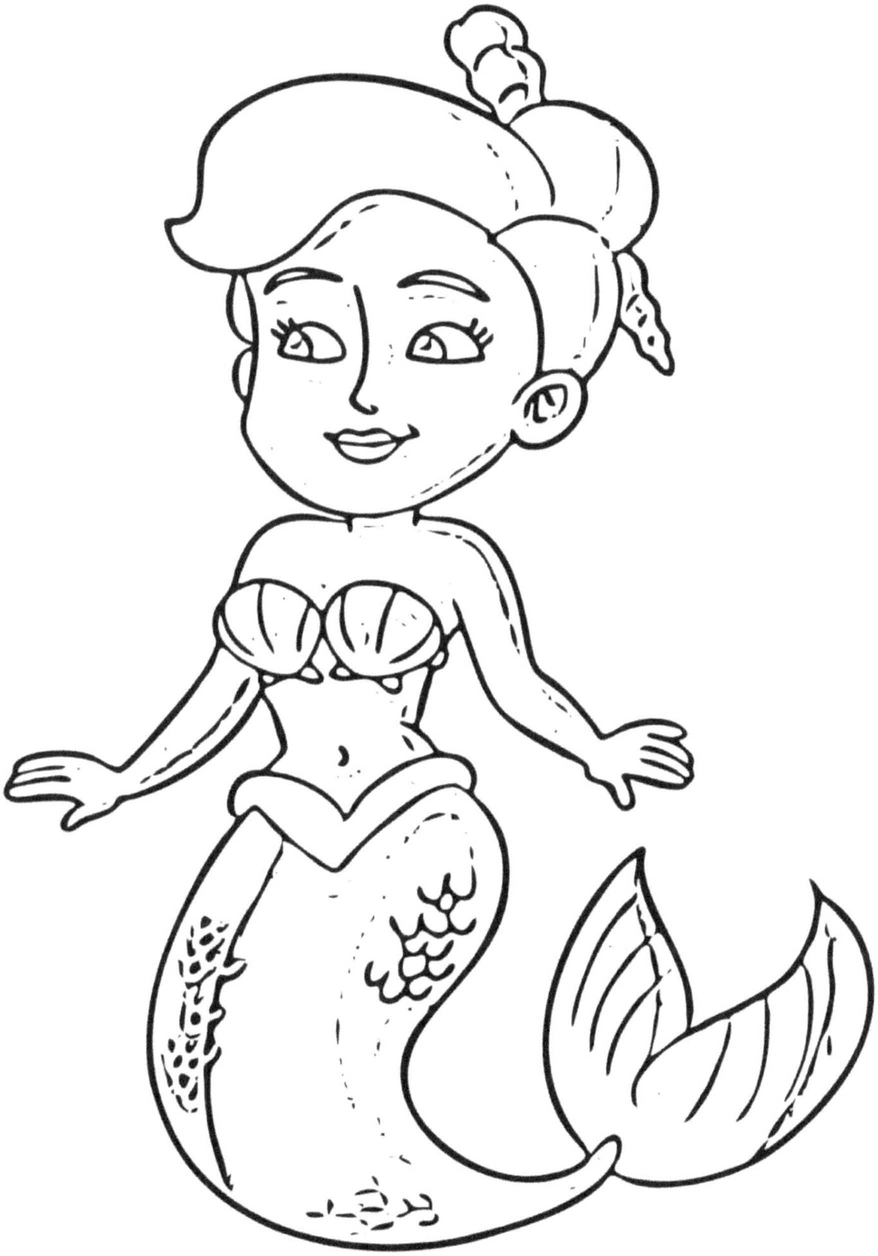

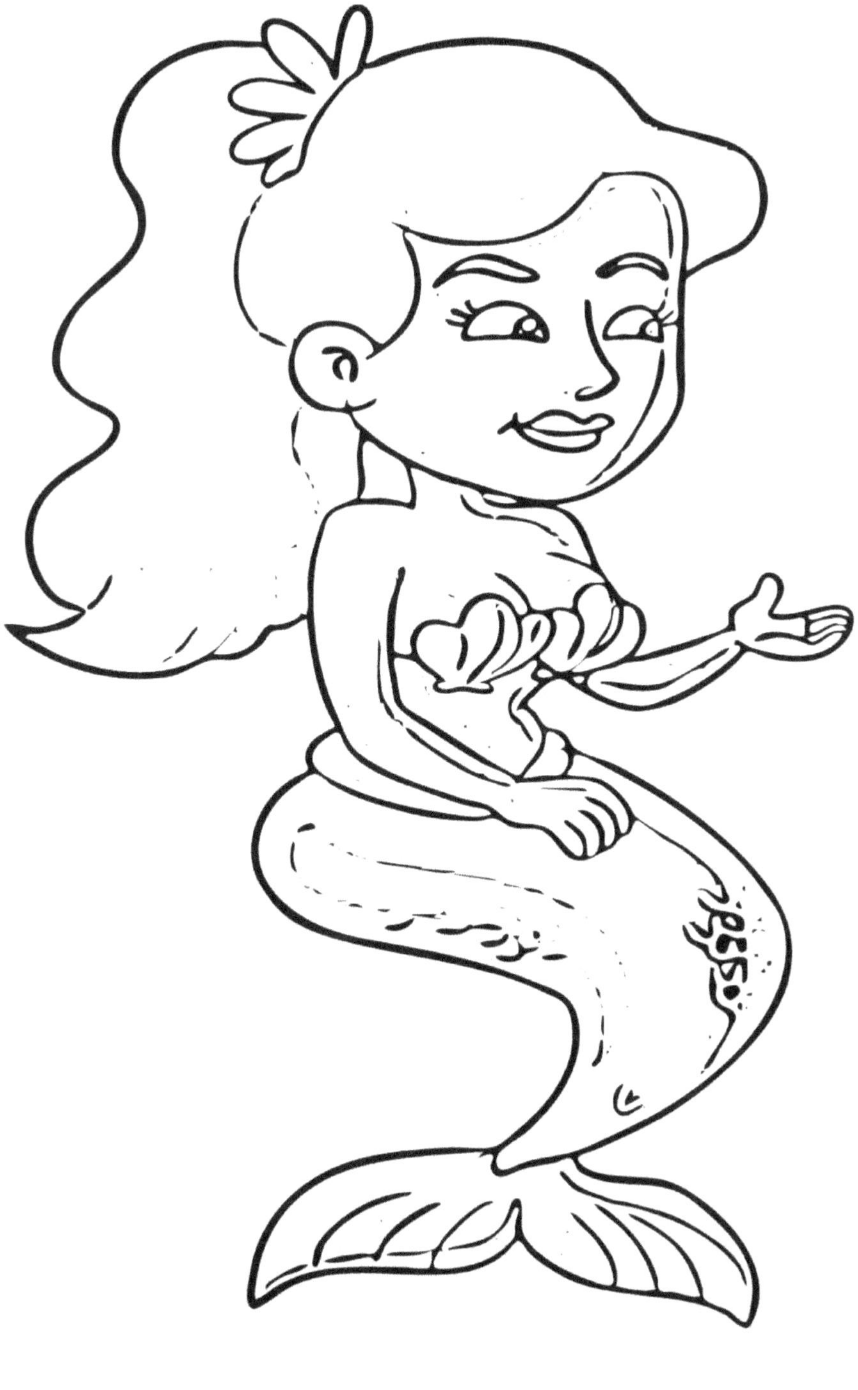

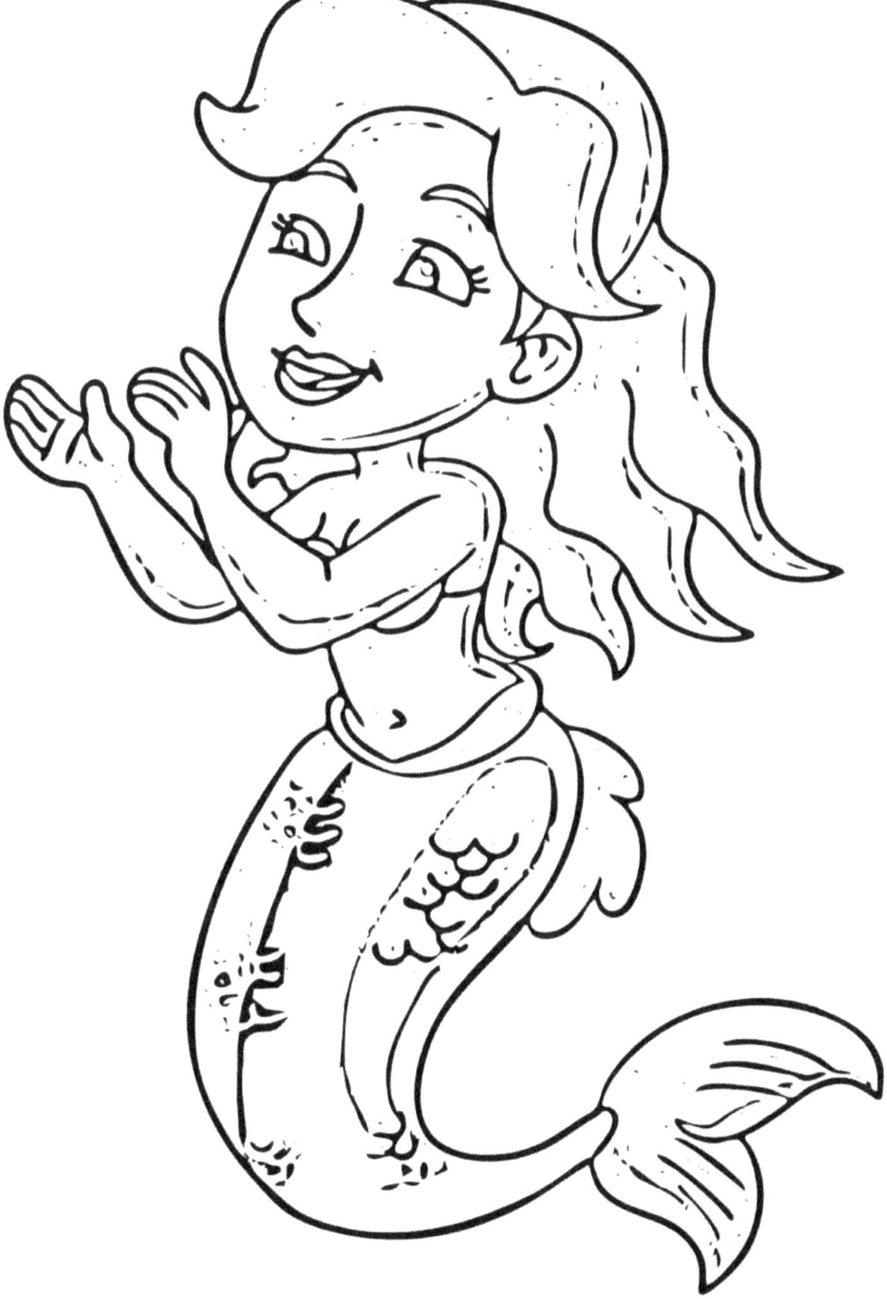

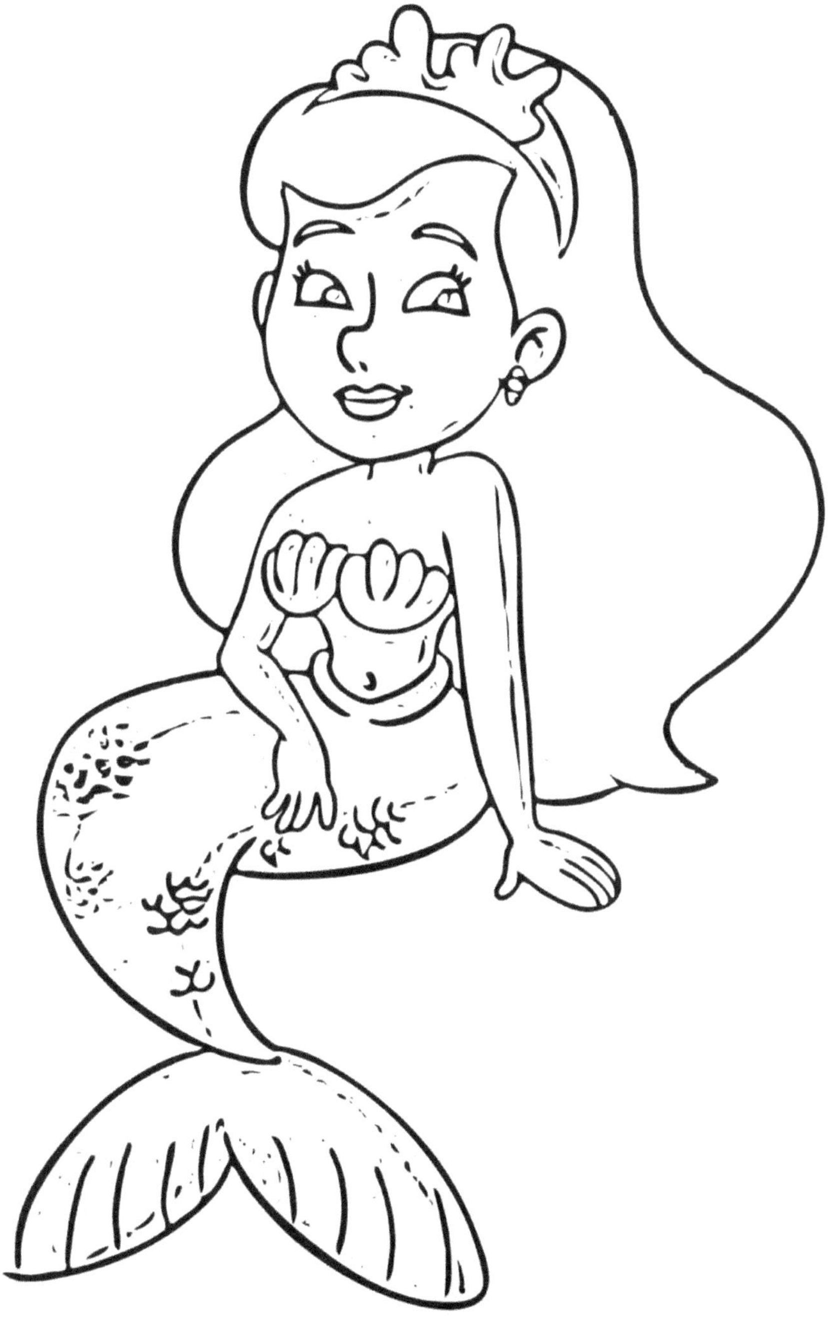

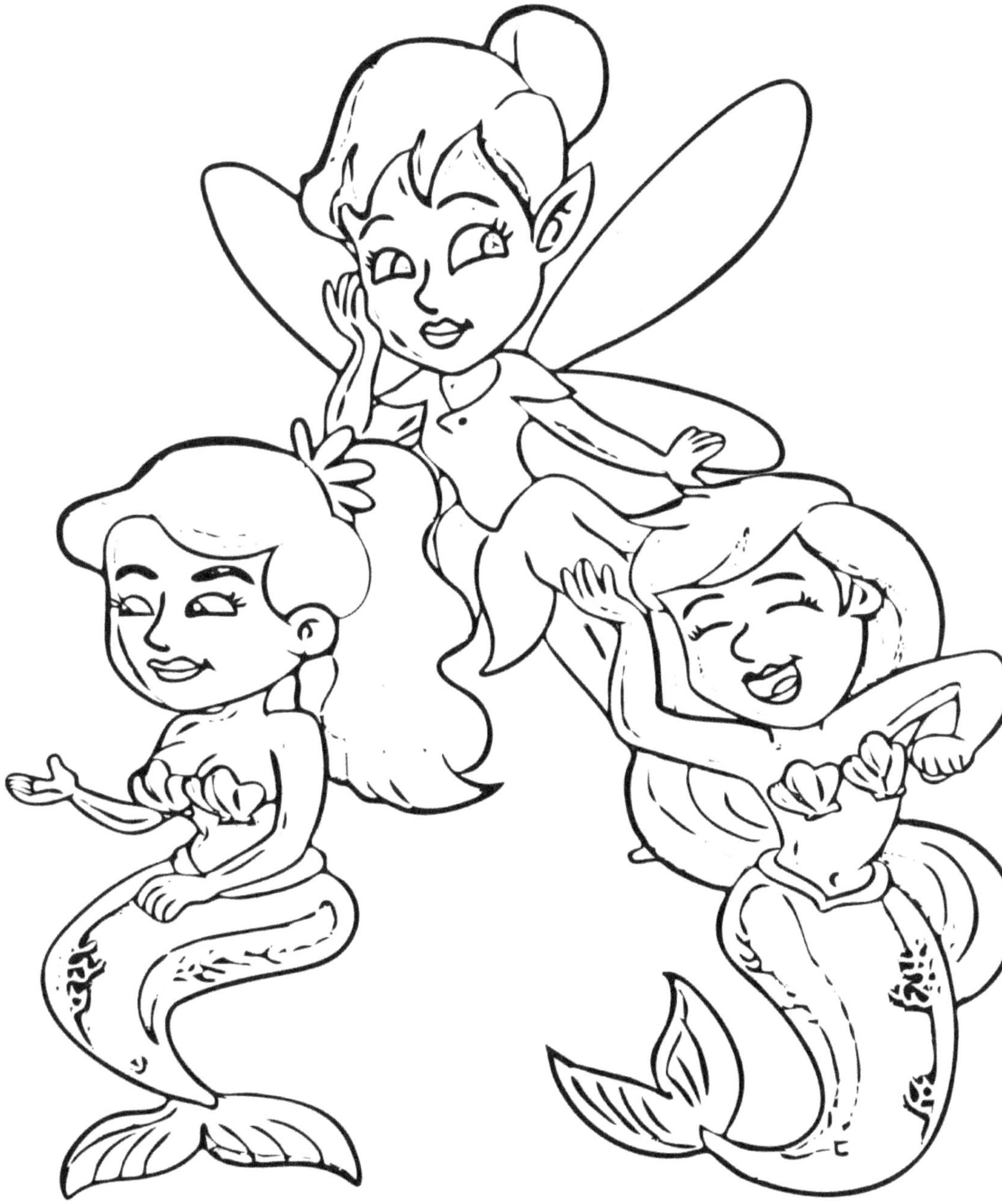

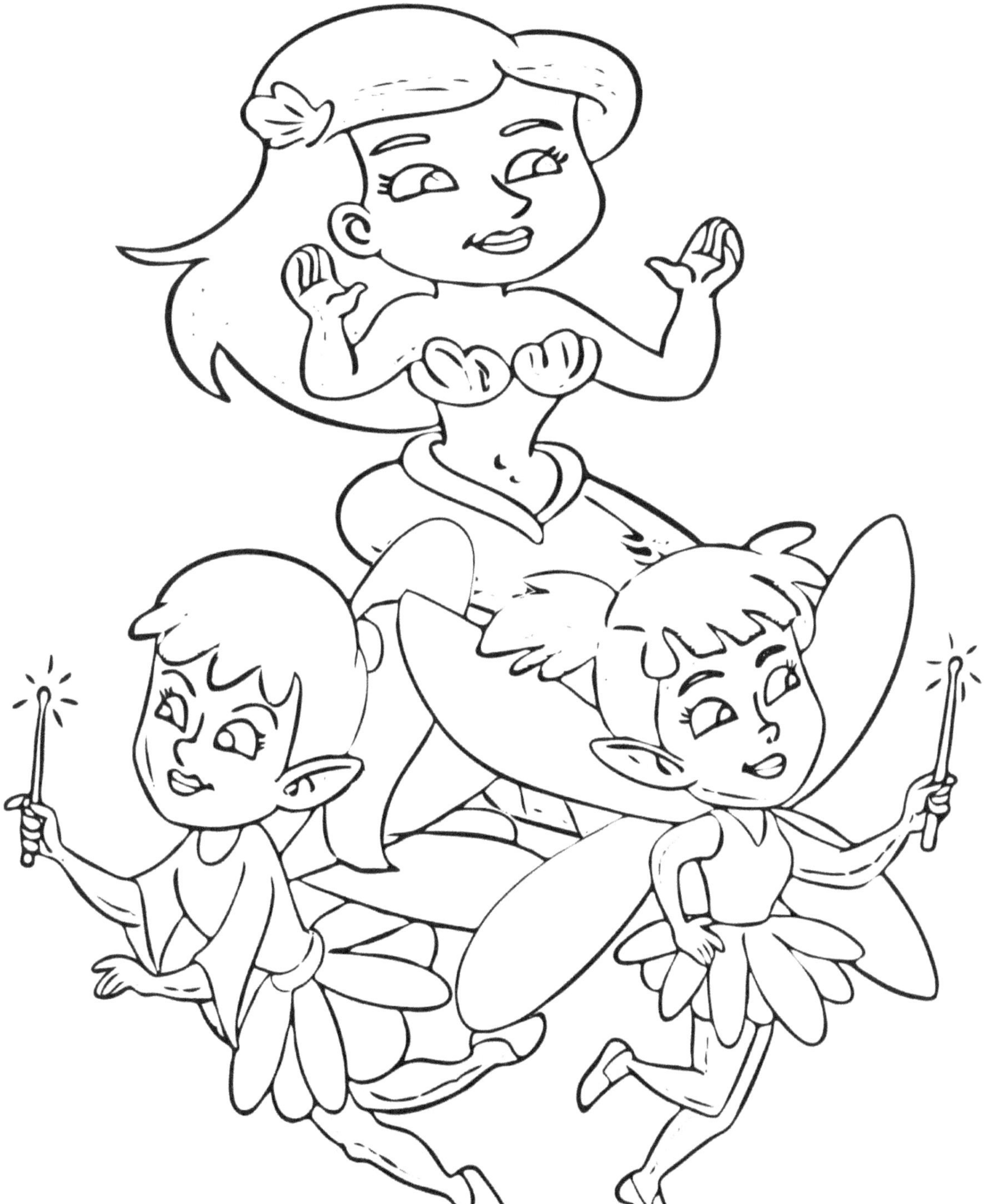

# SUPER CUTE KIDS
## Coloring Book

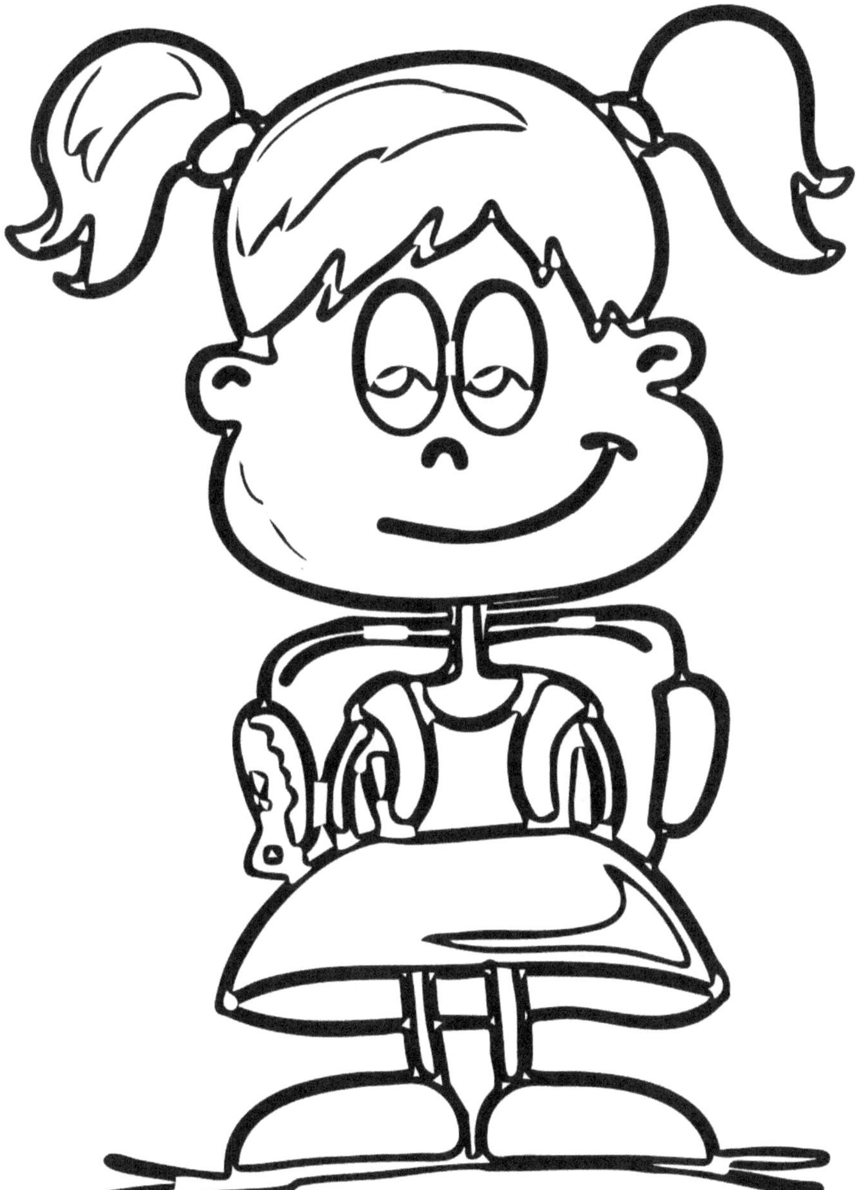

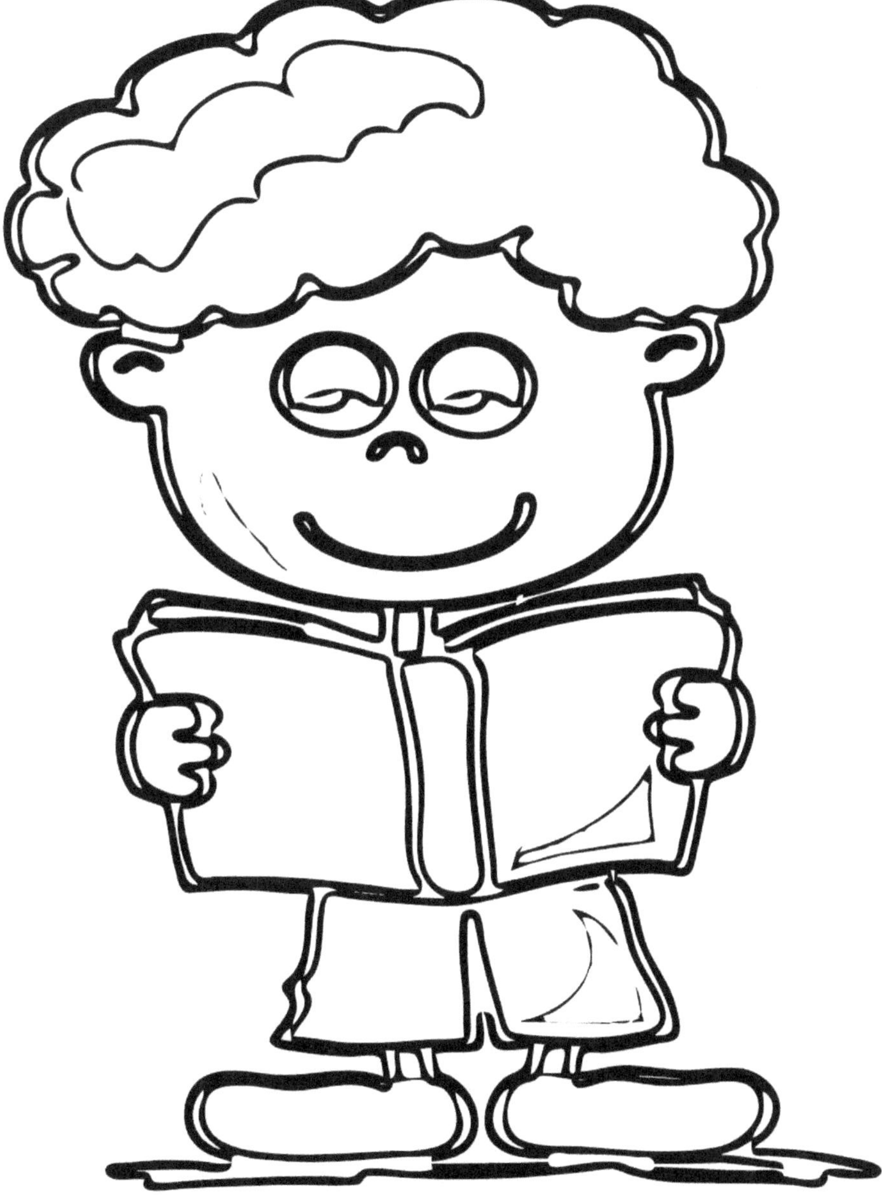

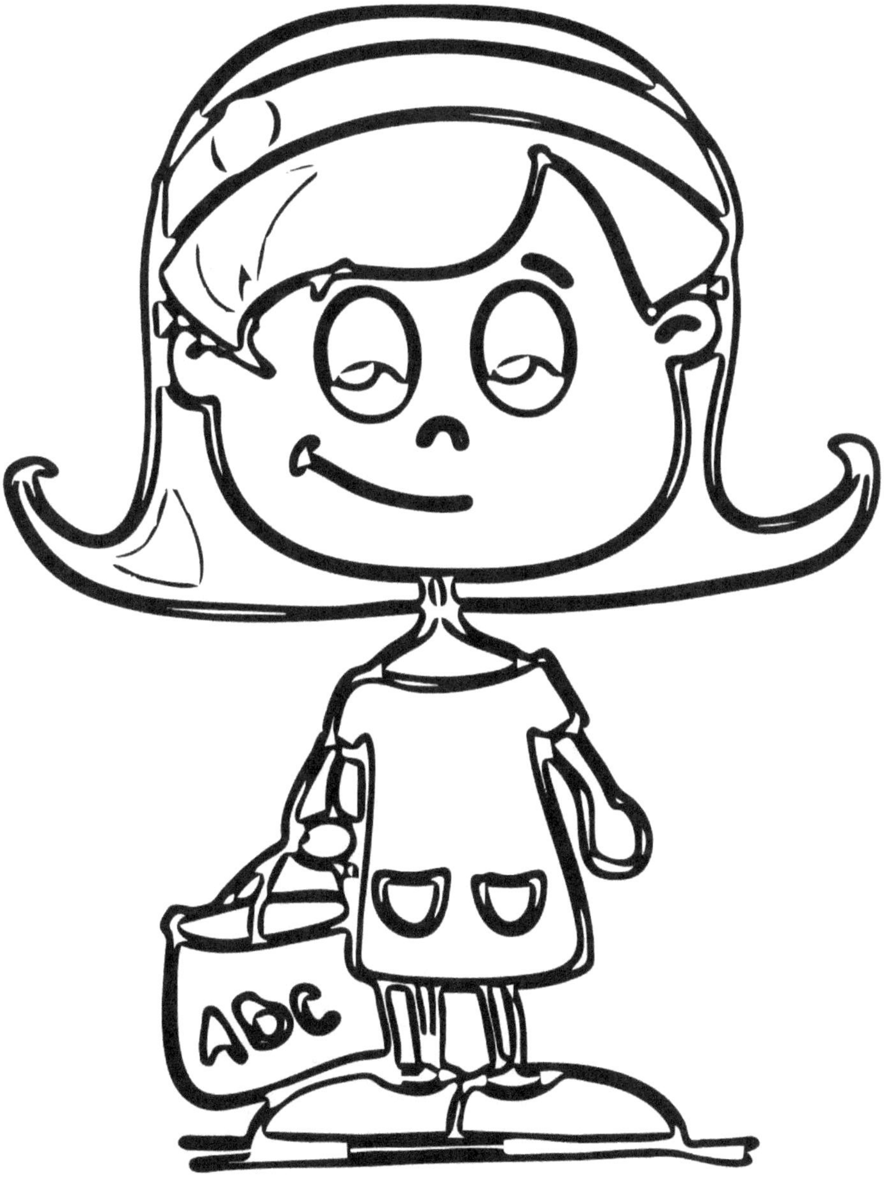
ABC

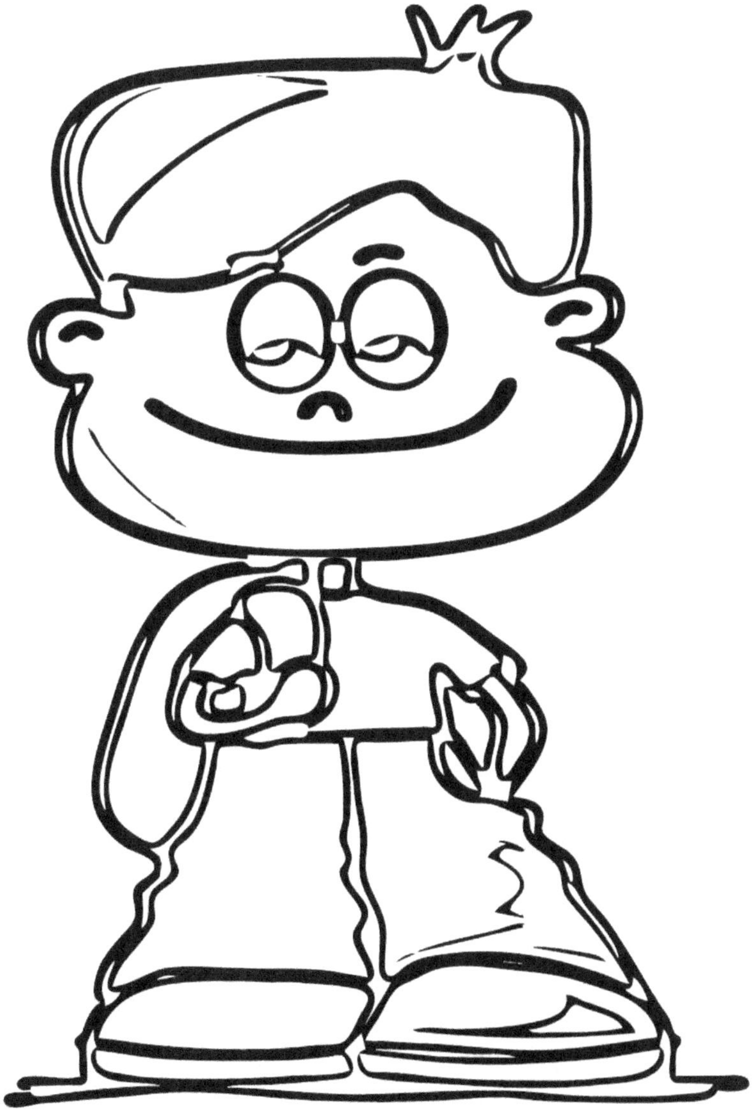

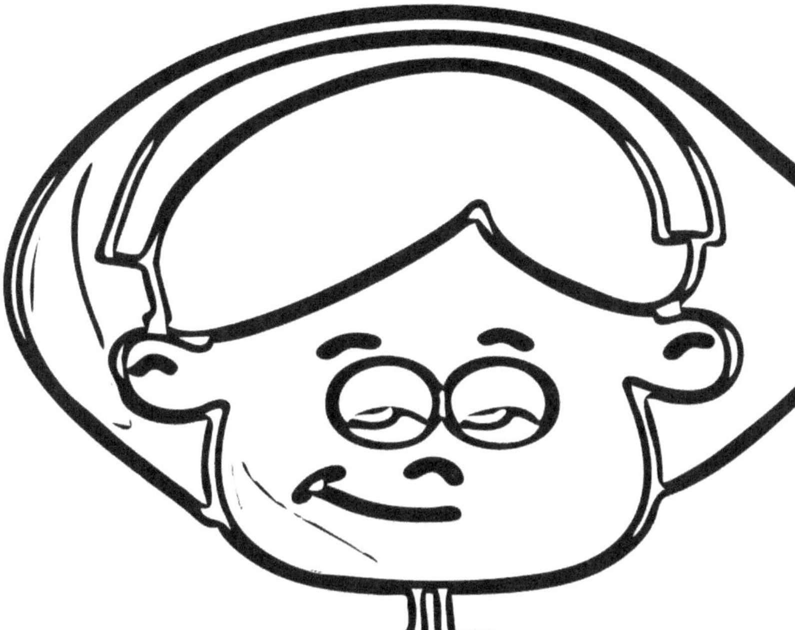

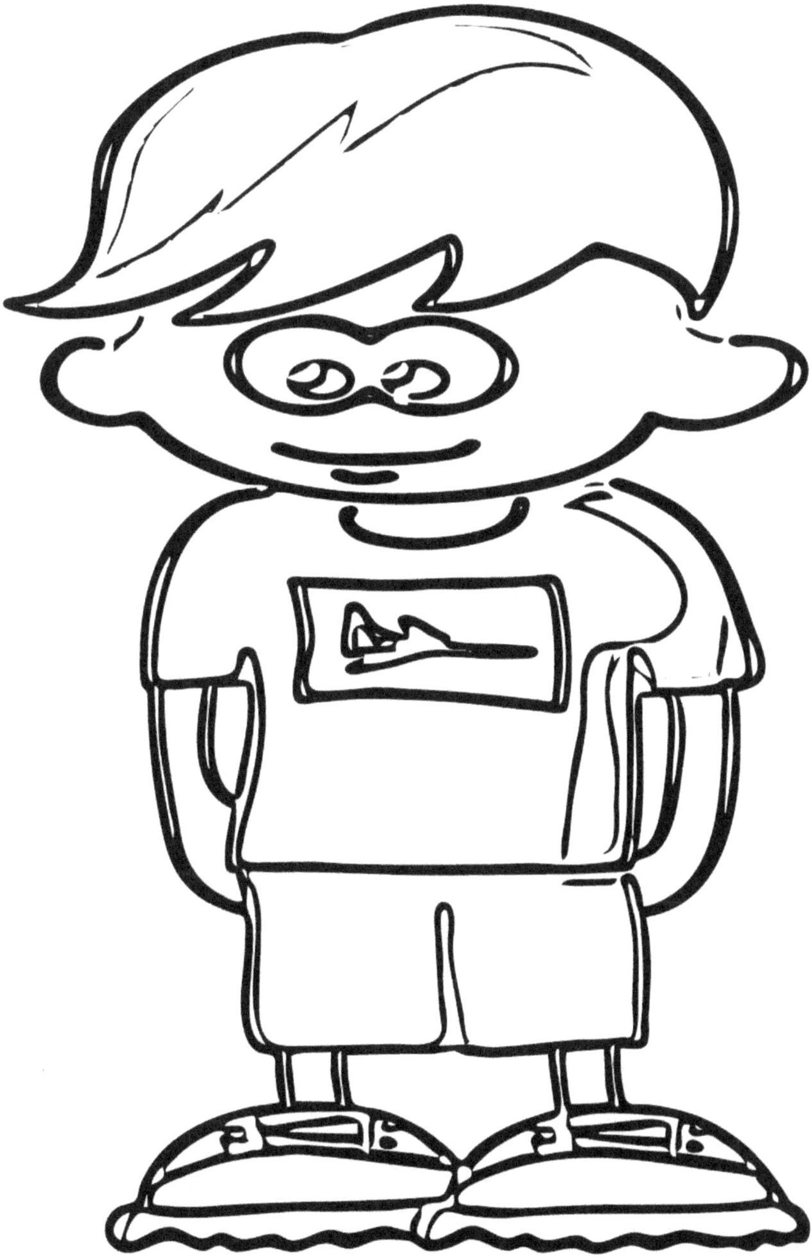

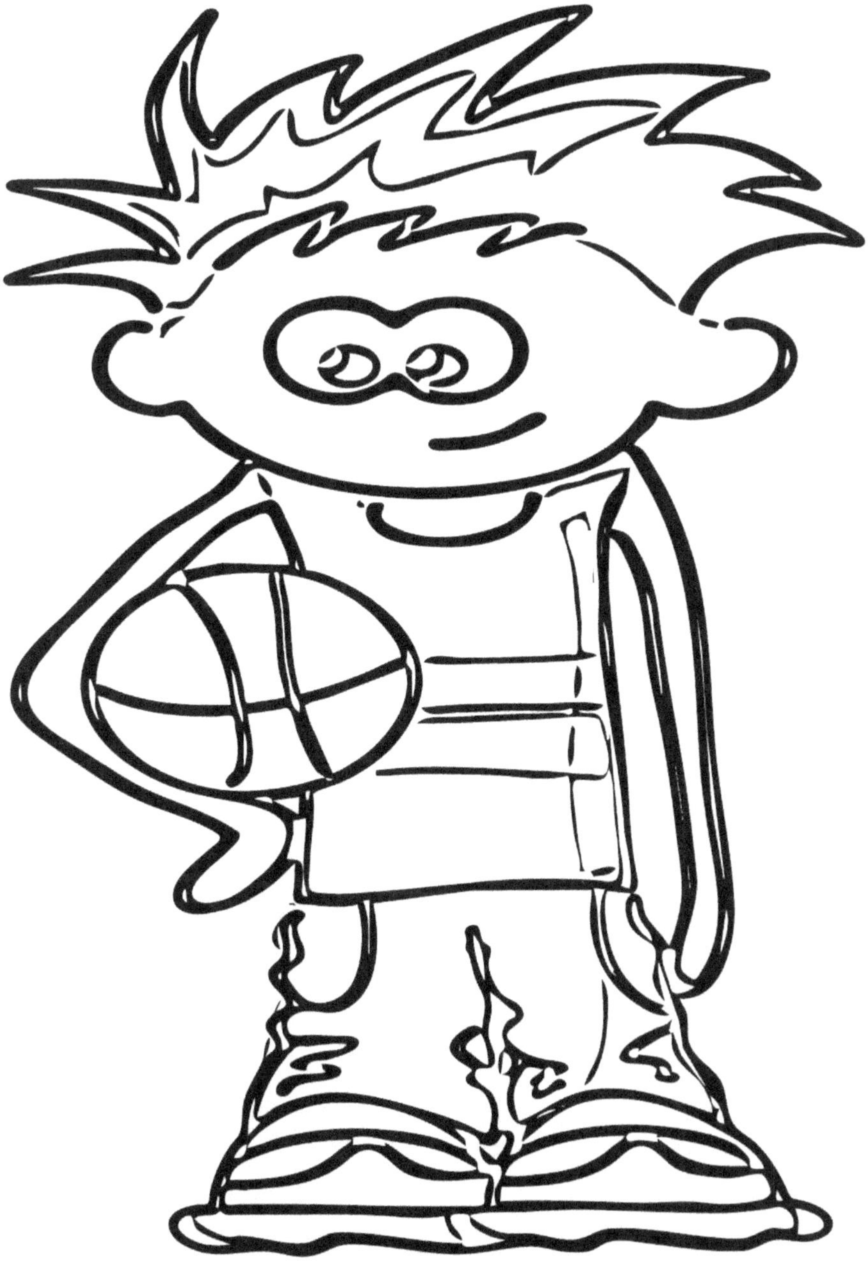

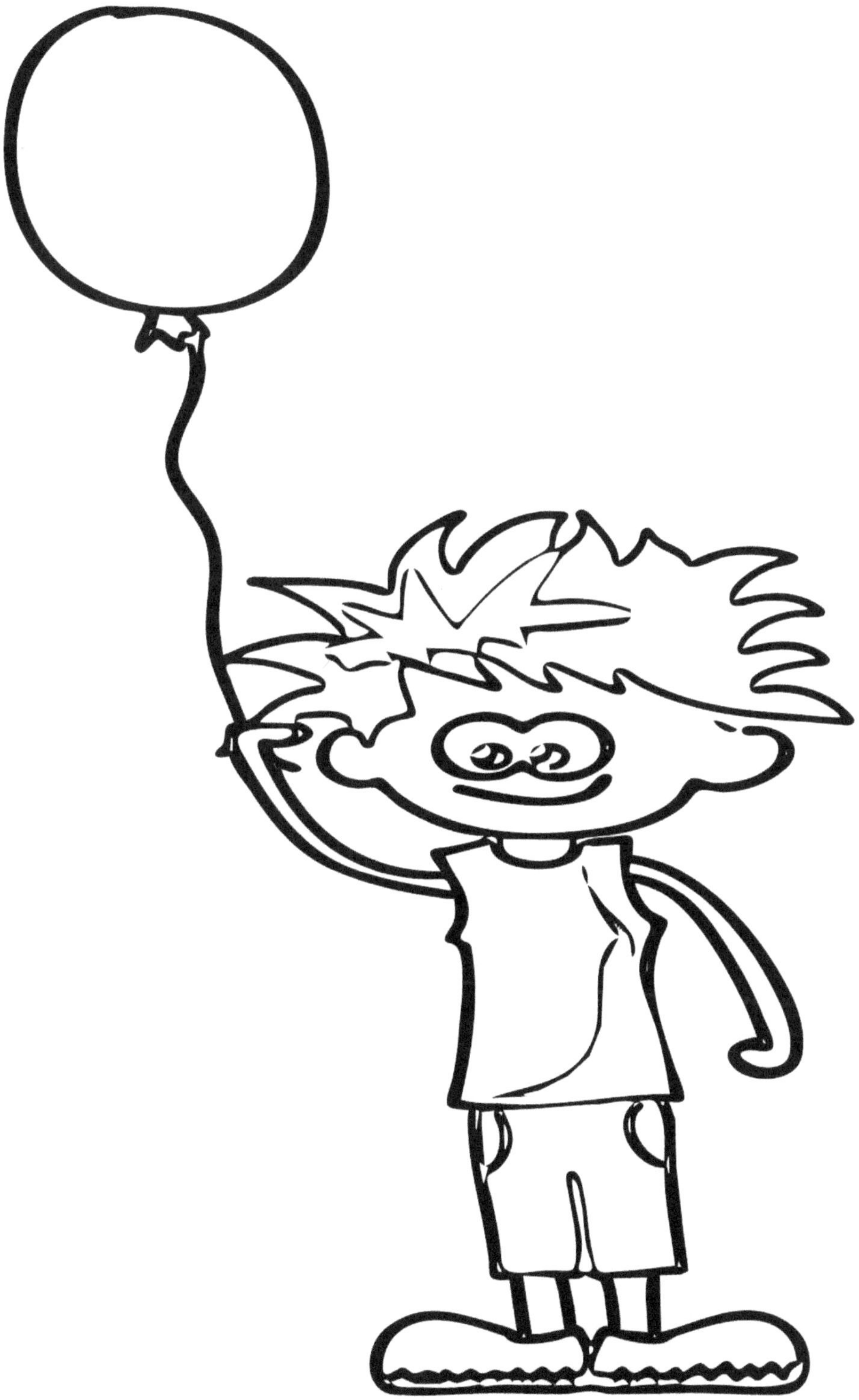

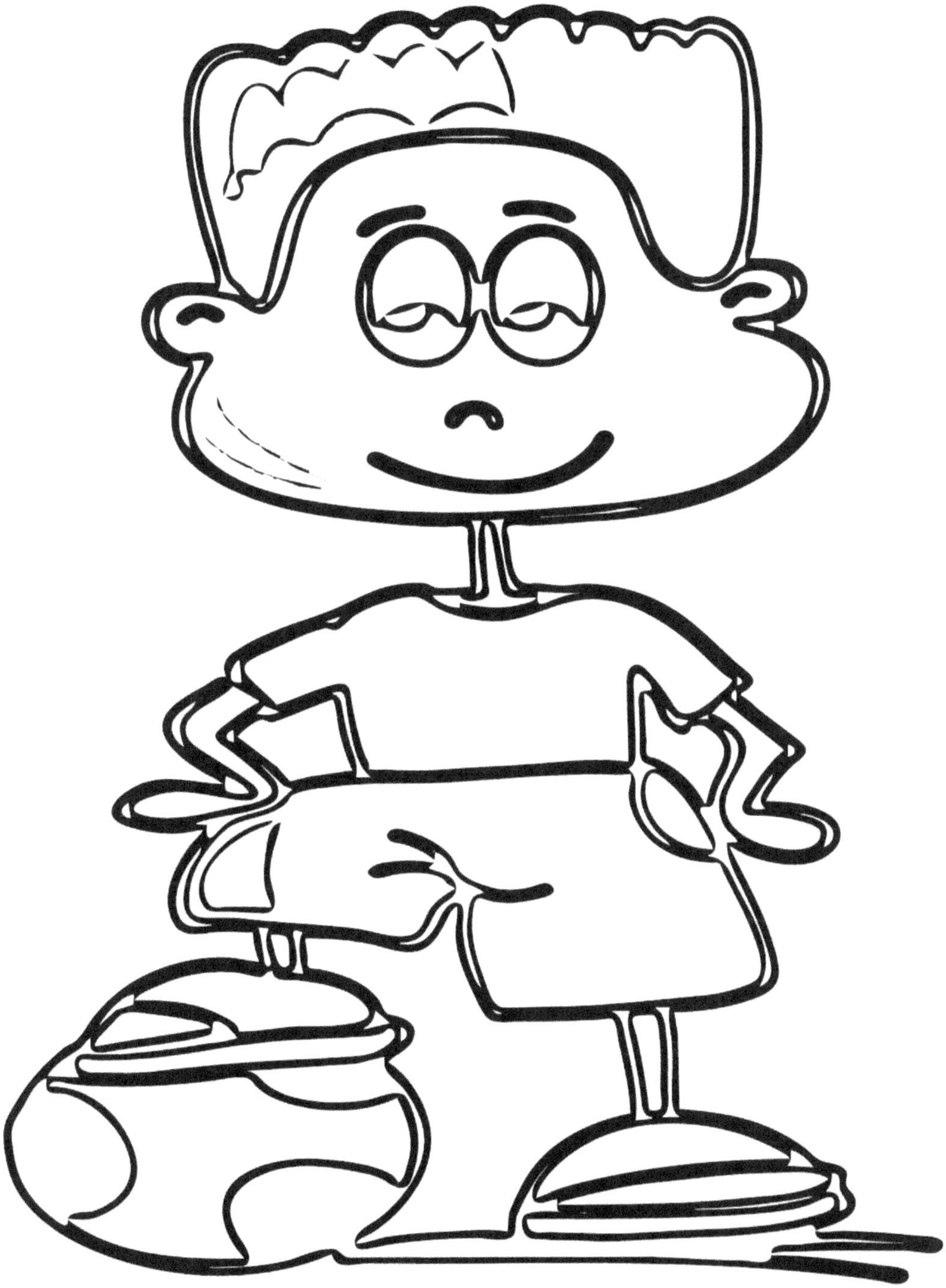

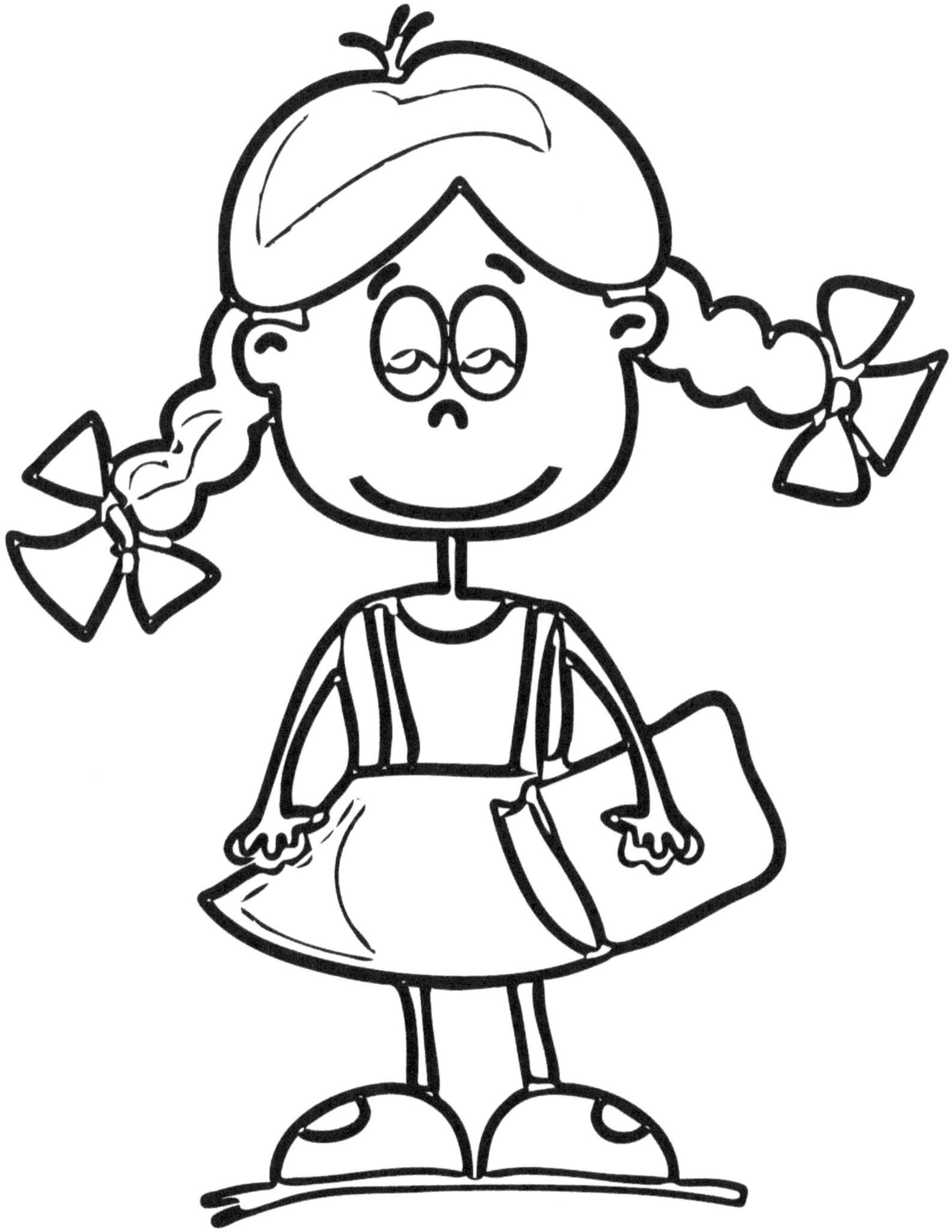

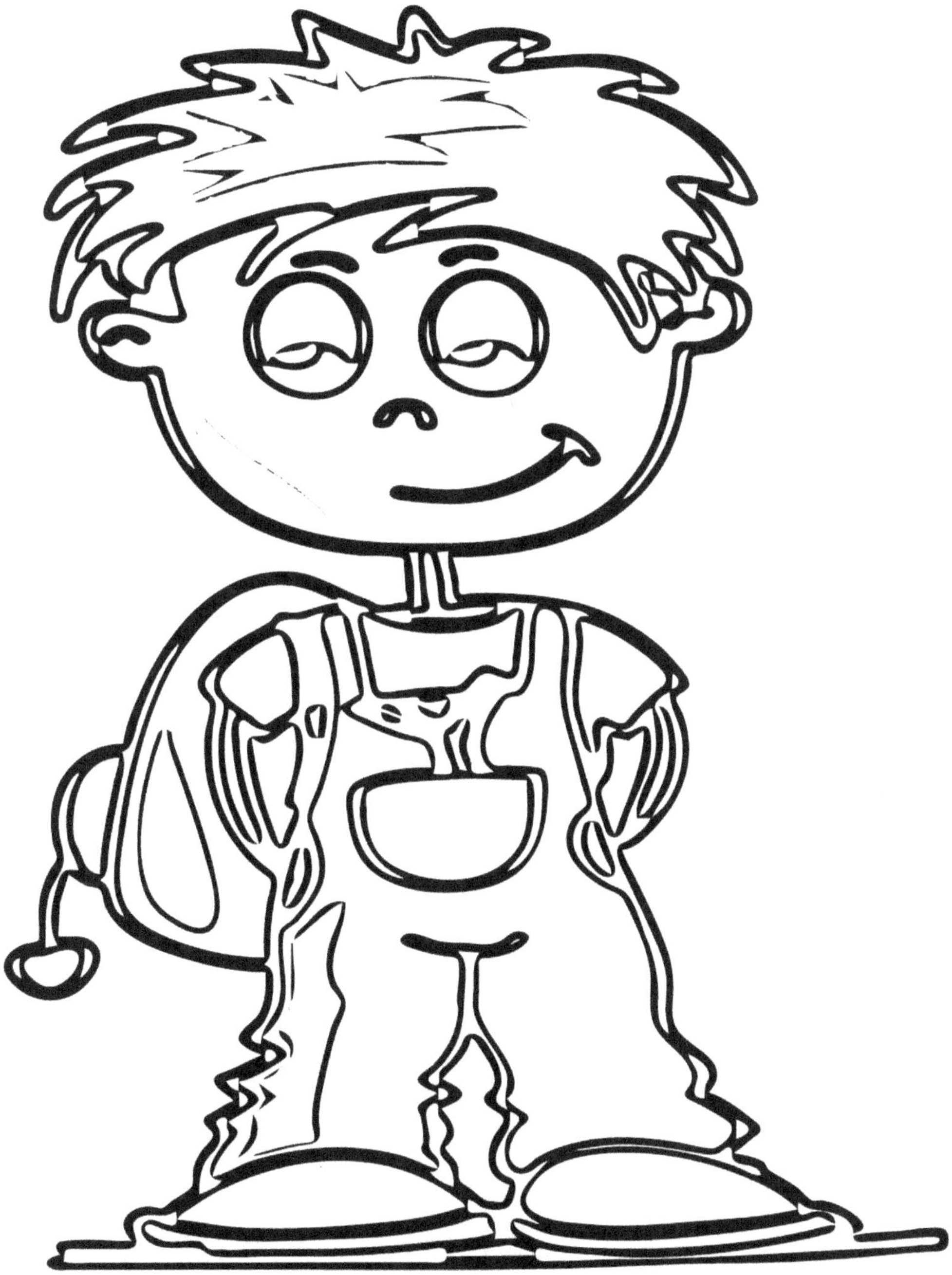

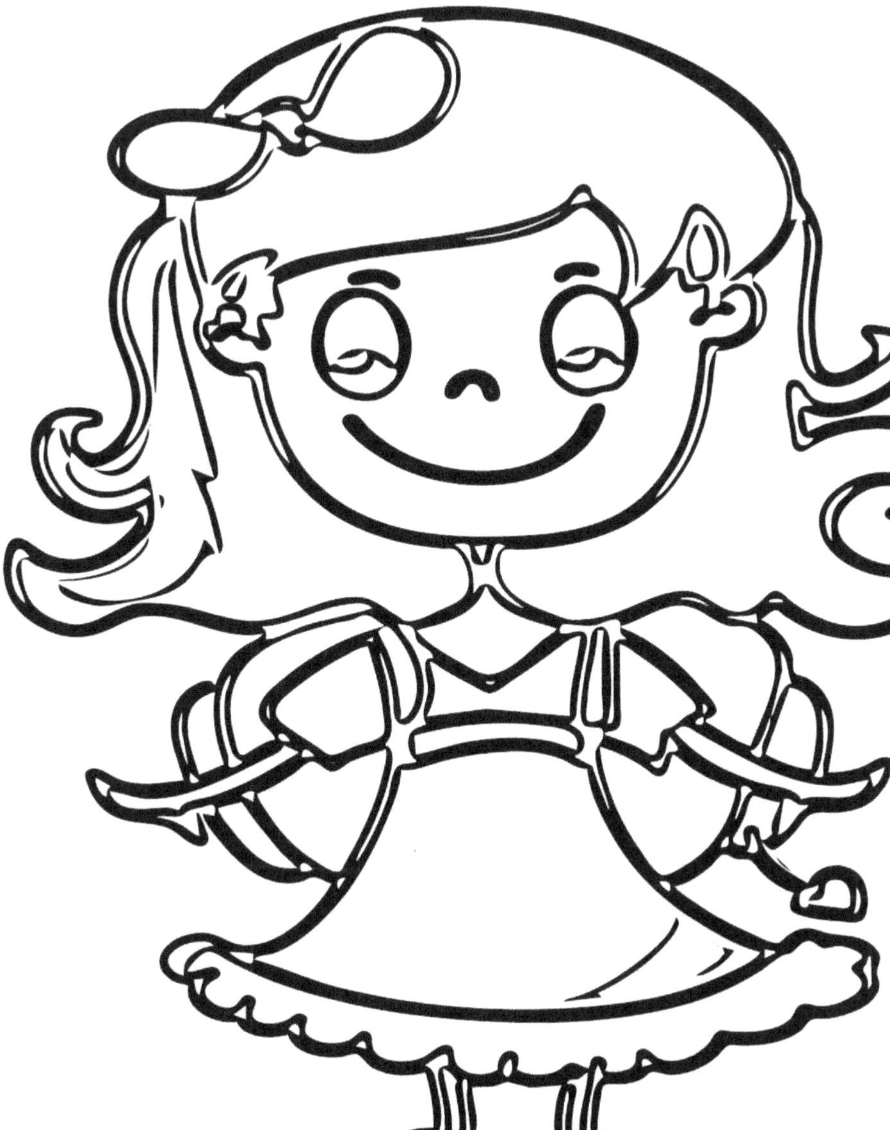

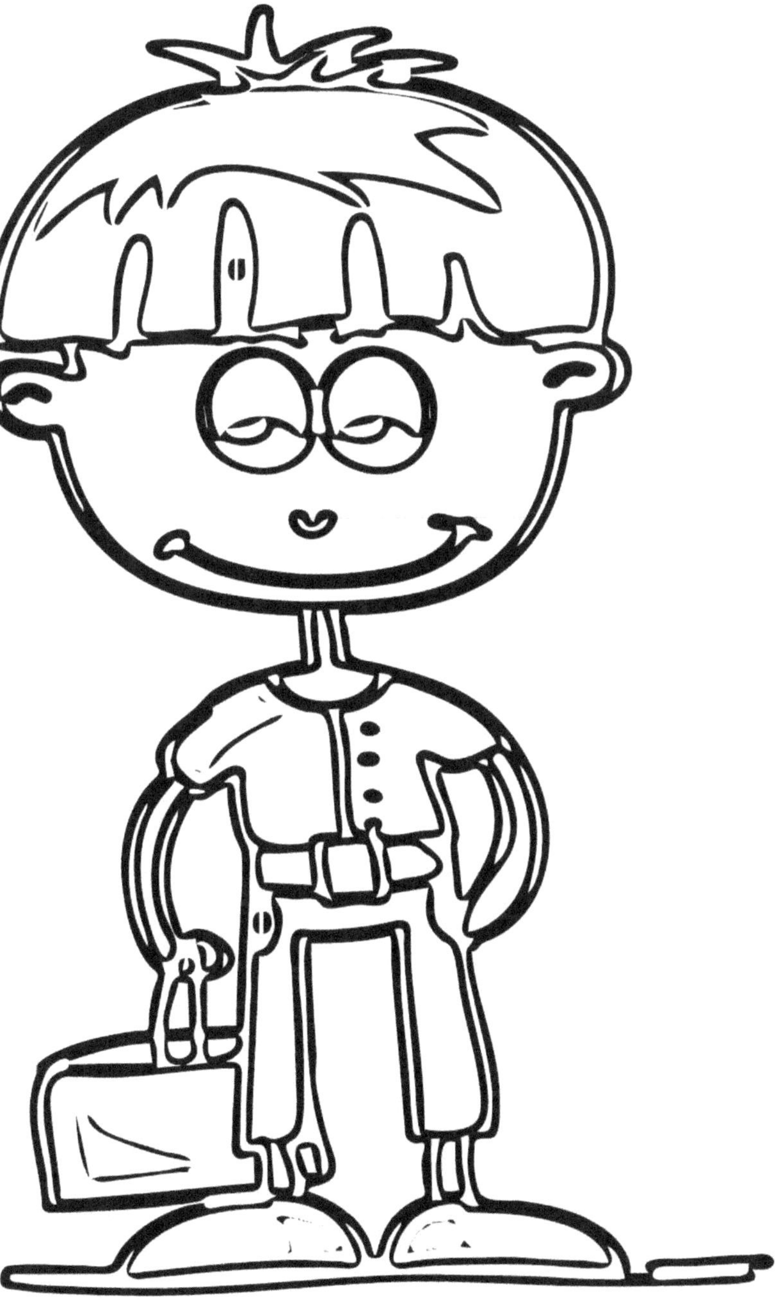

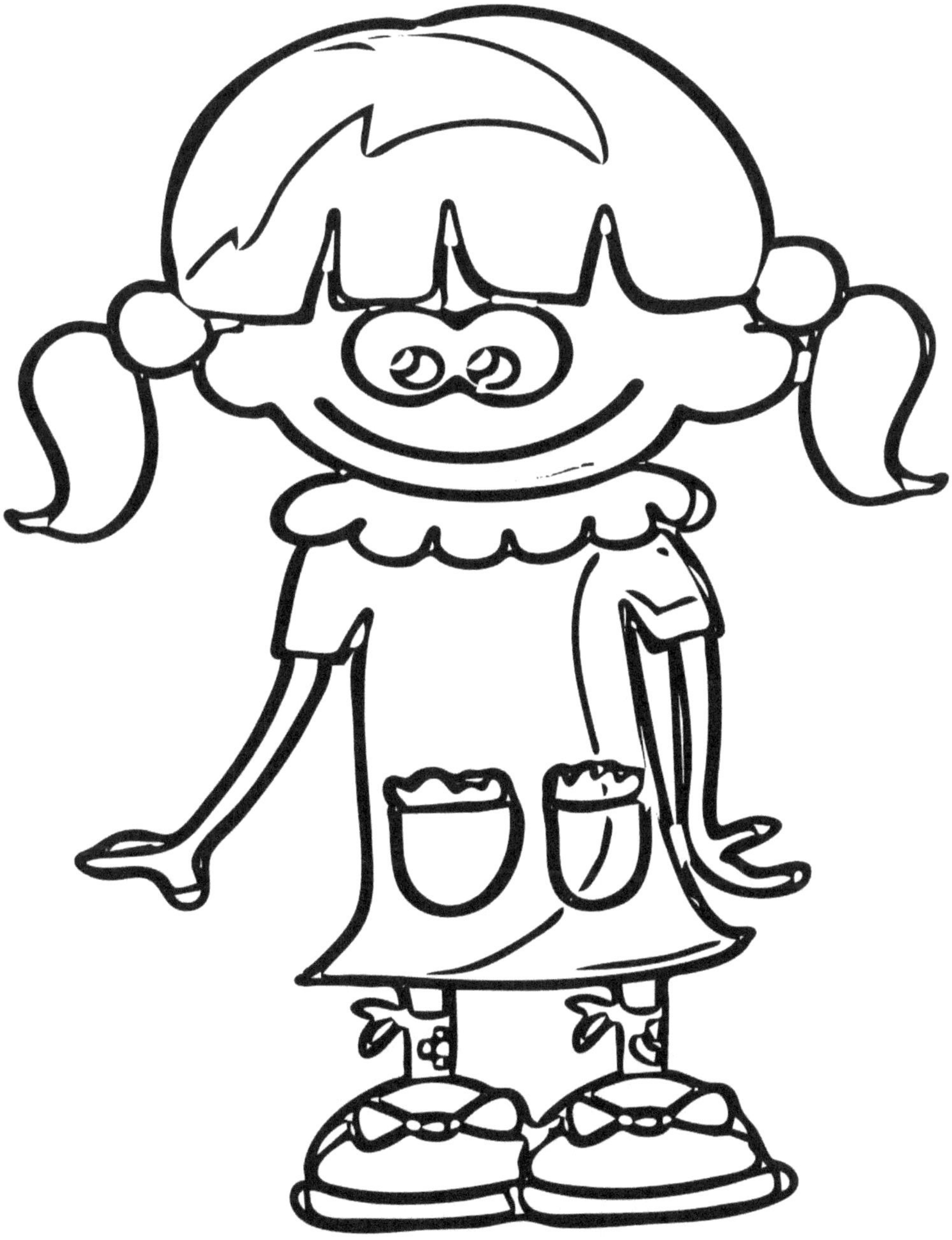

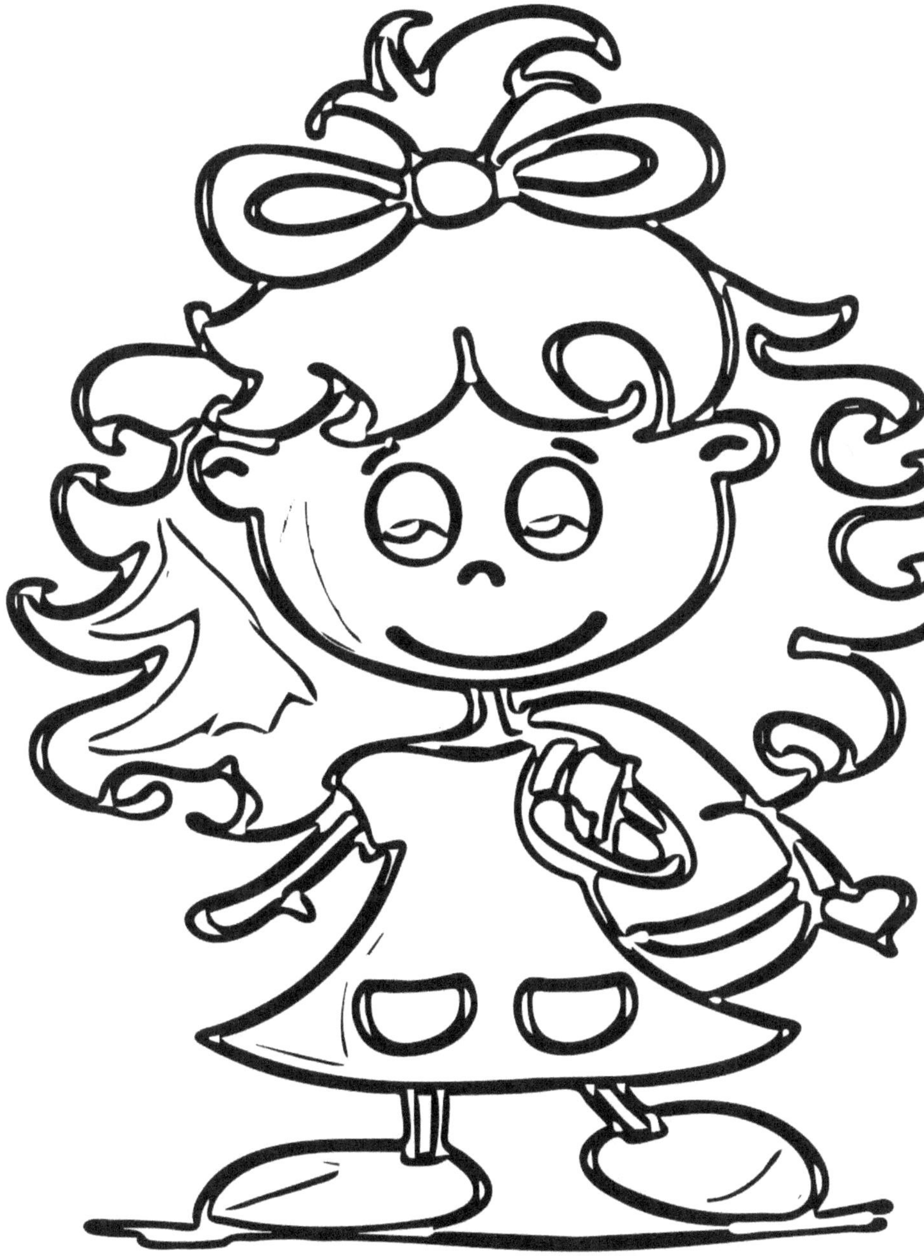

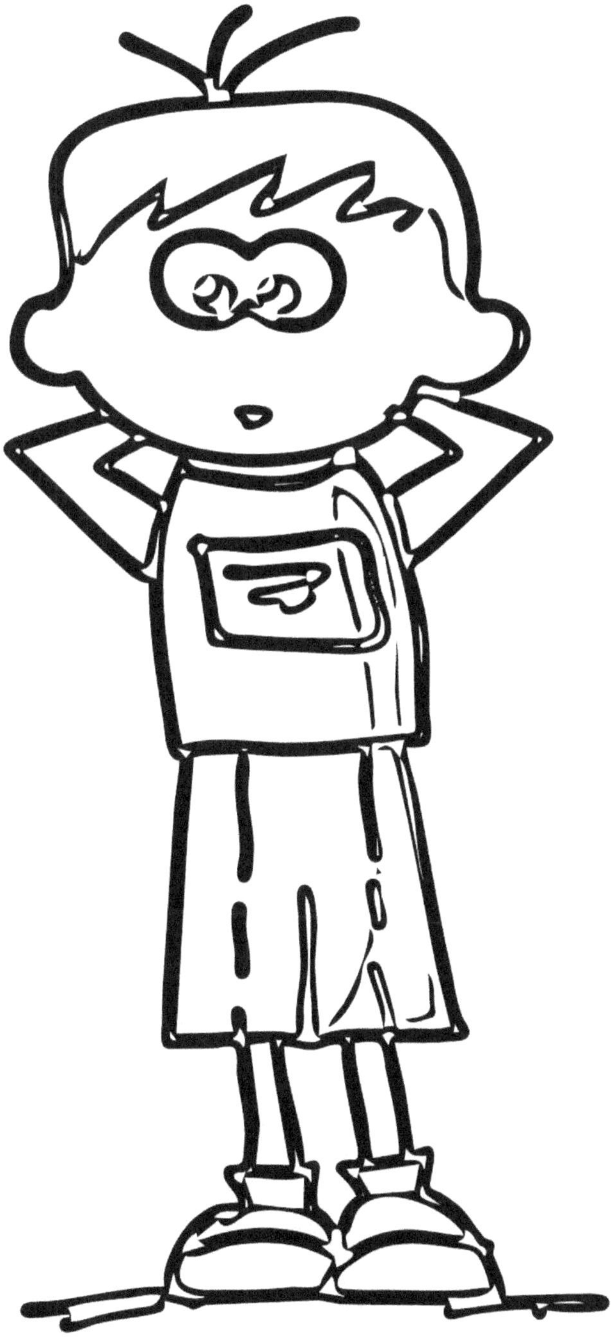

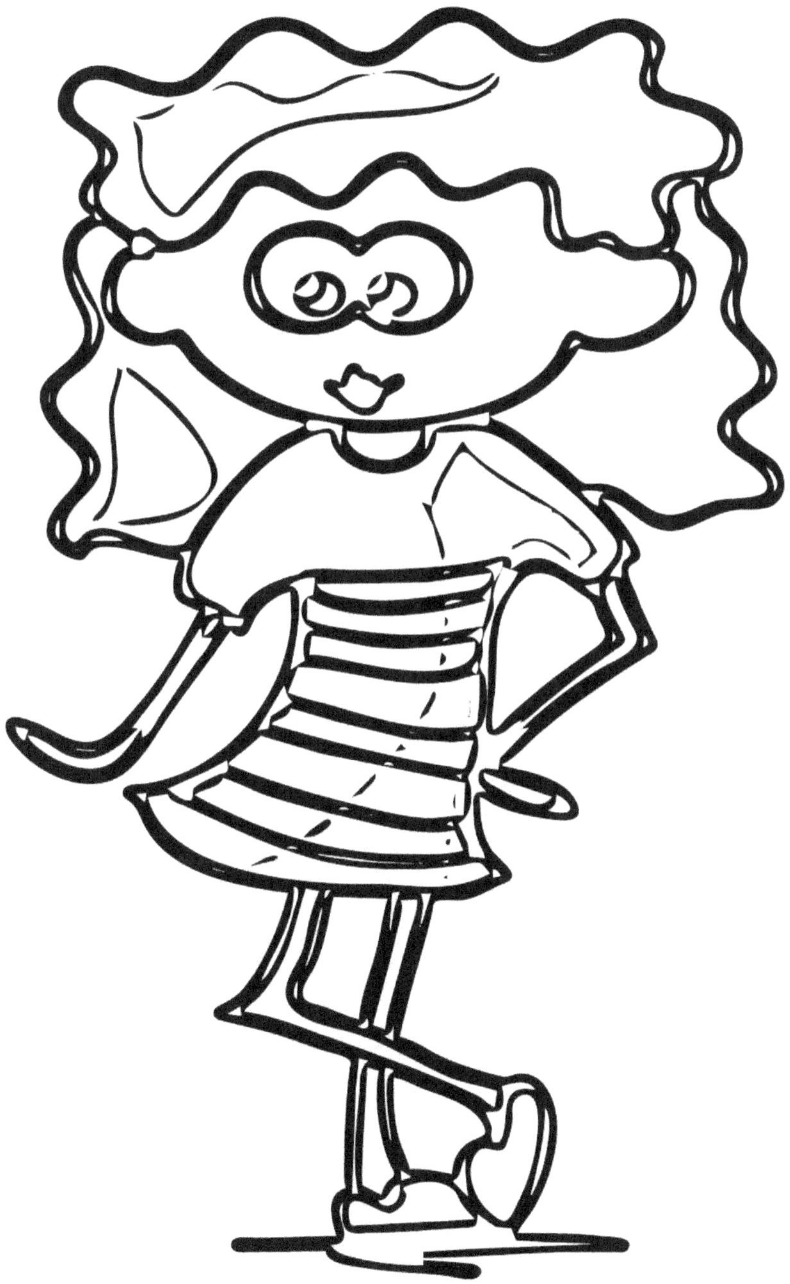

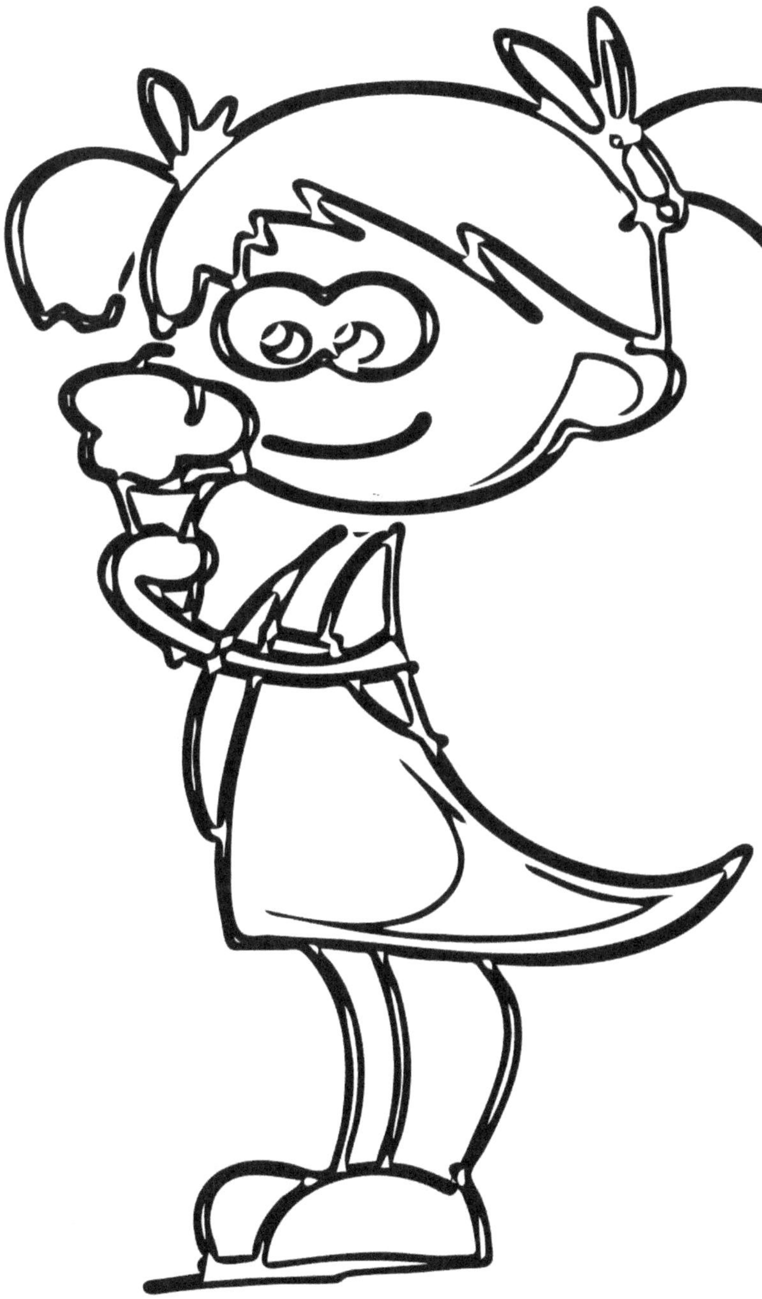

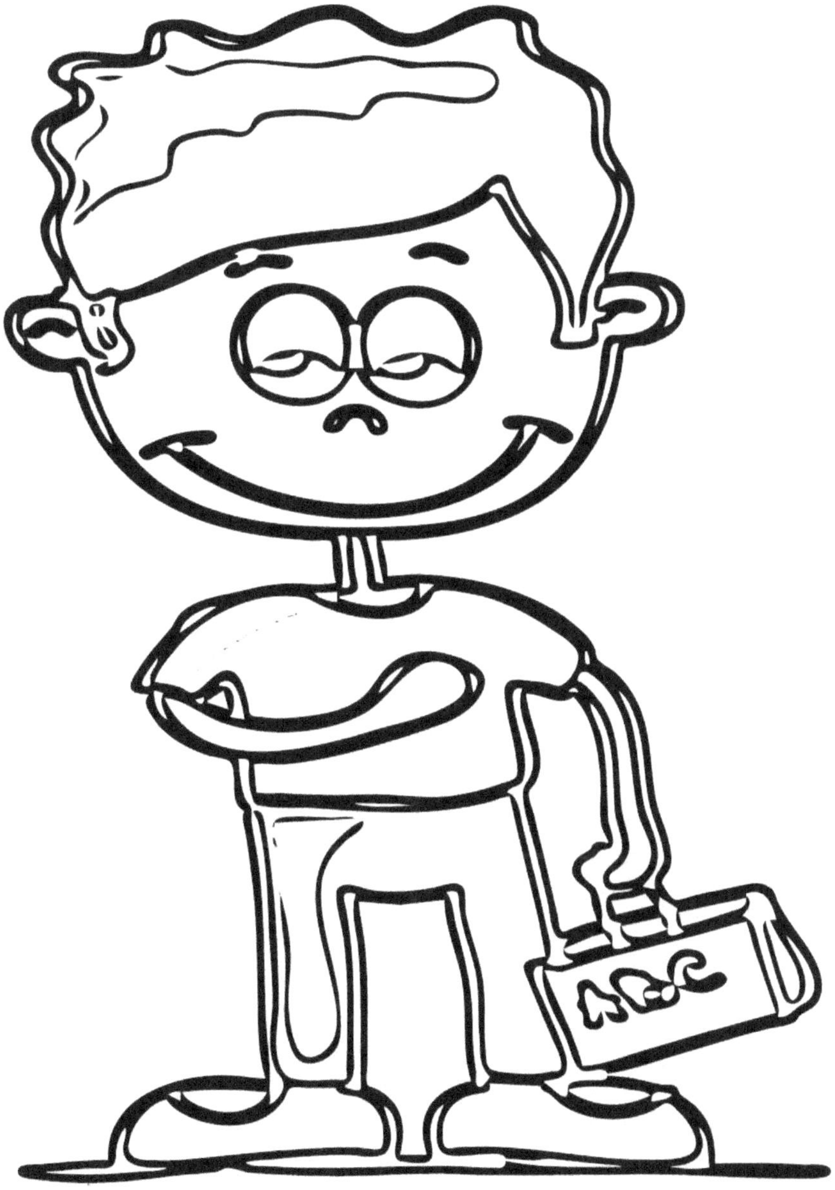
ABC

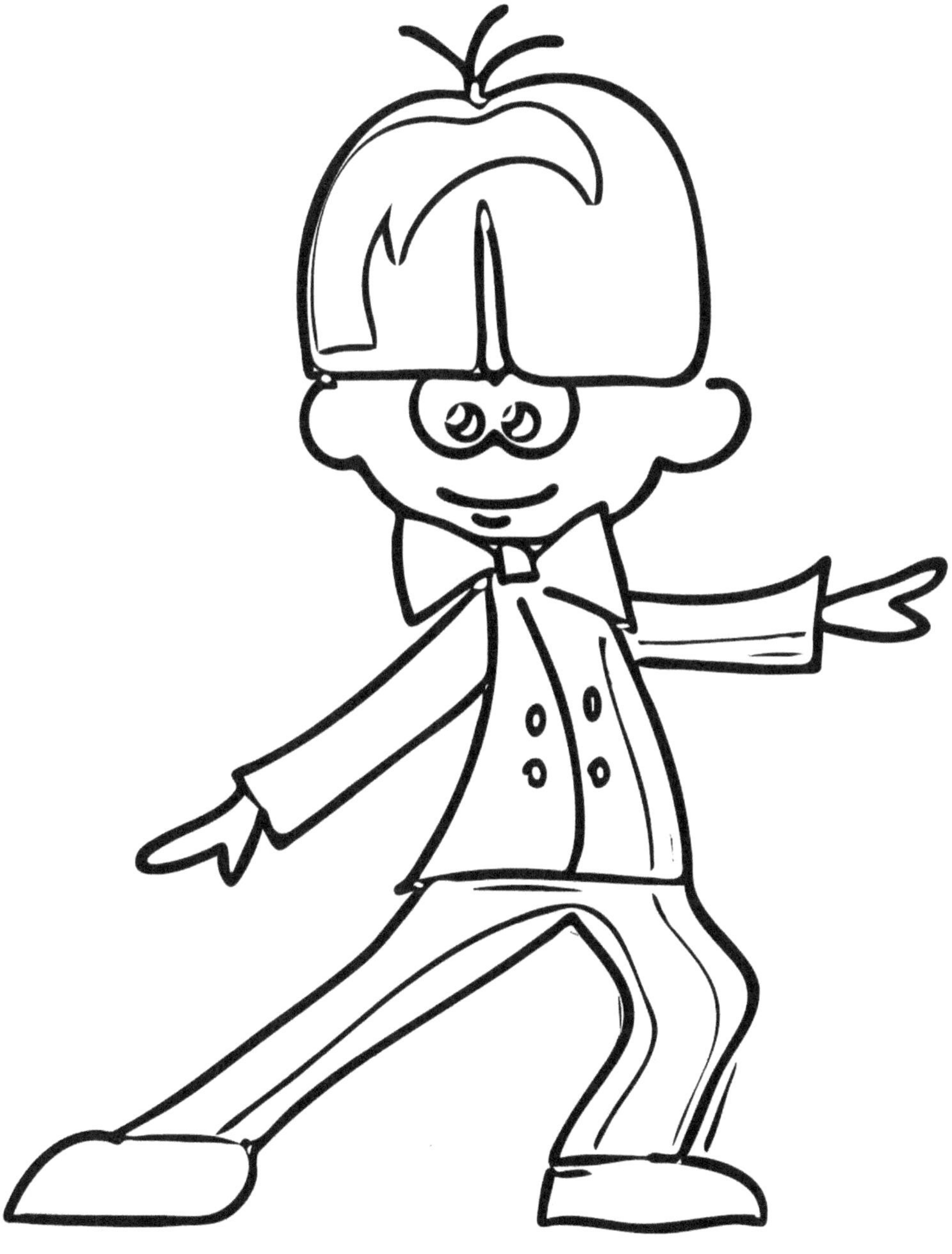

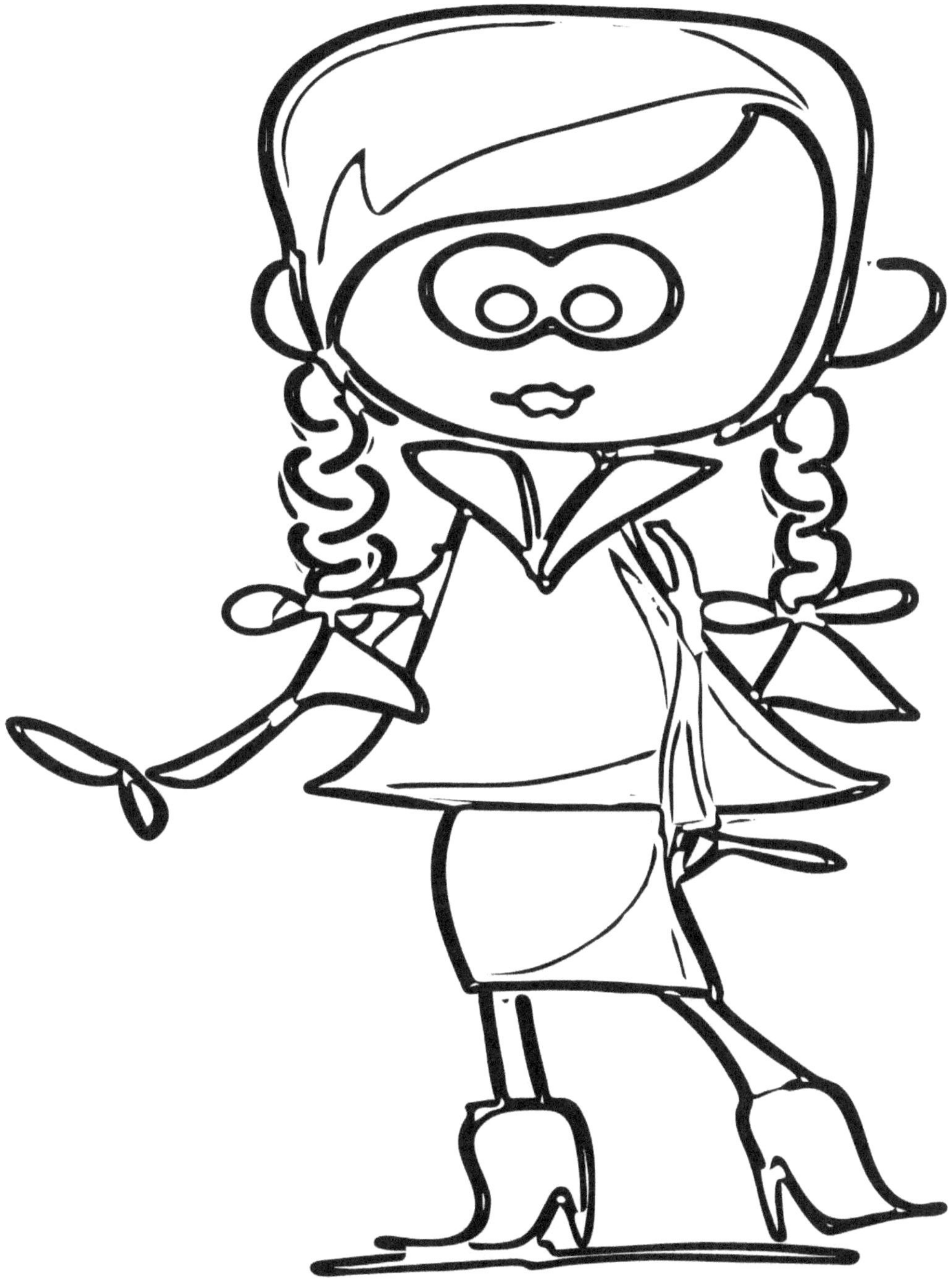

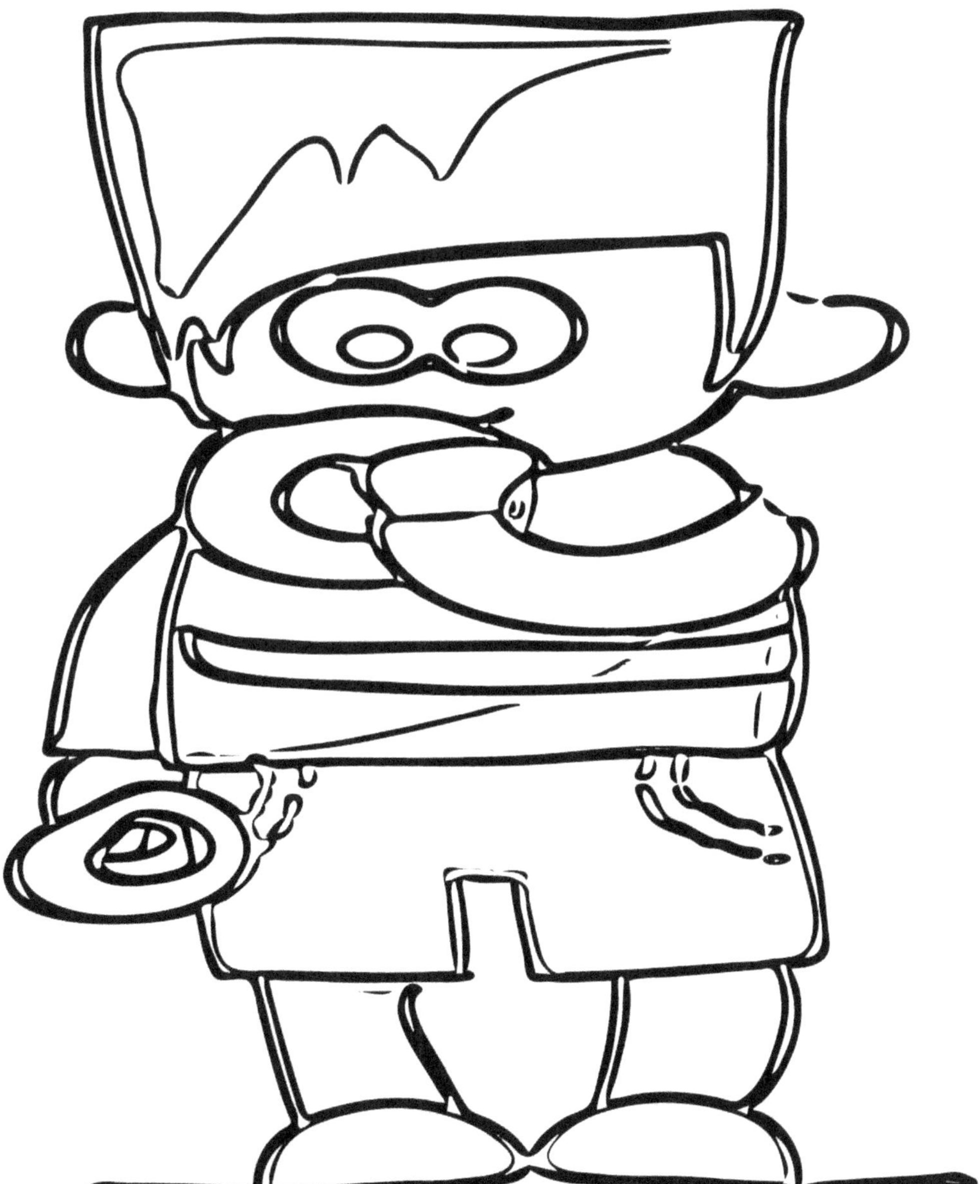

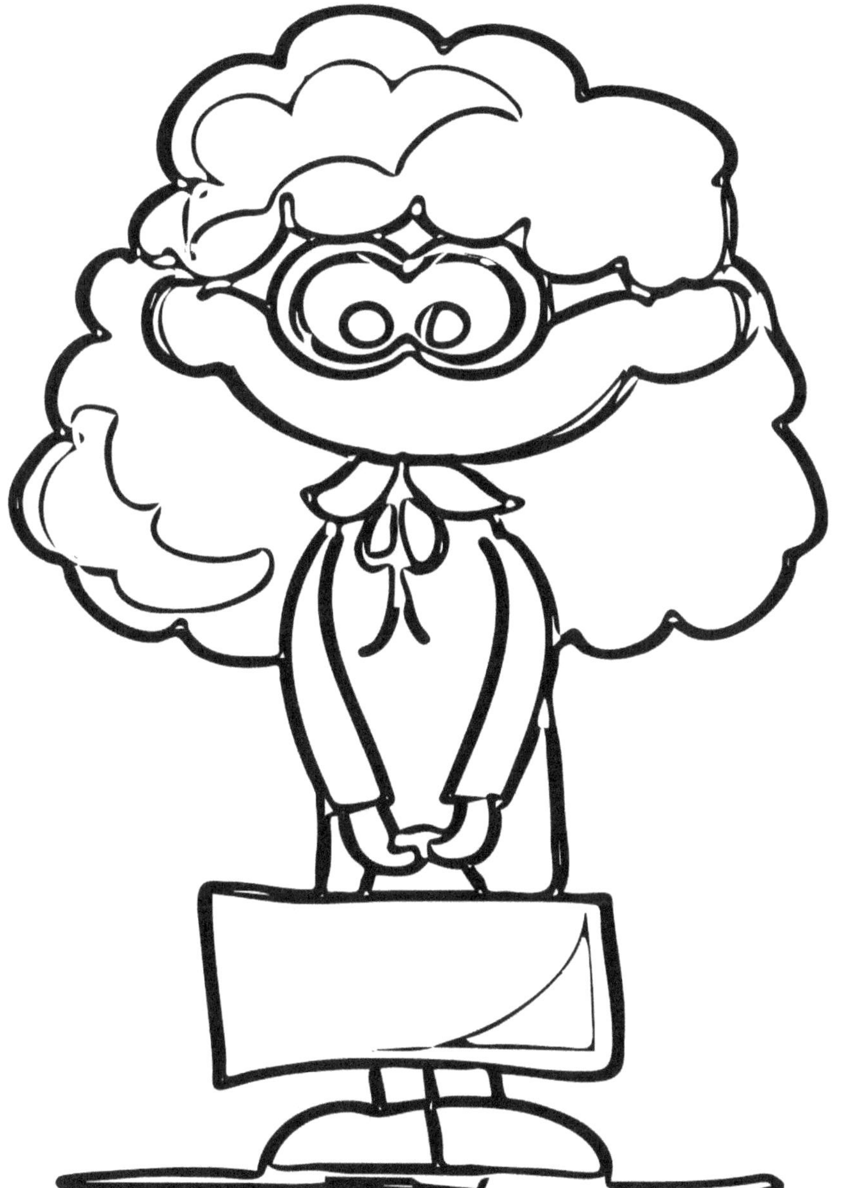

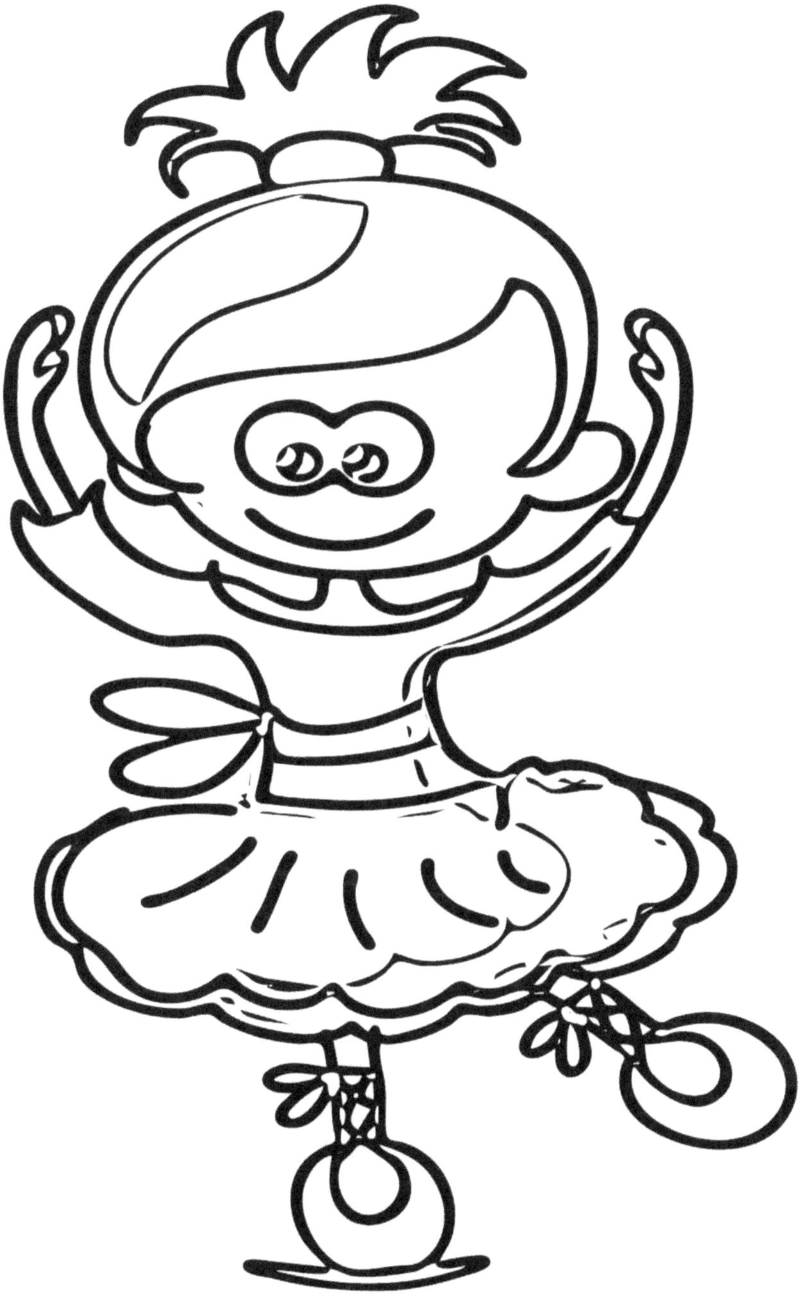

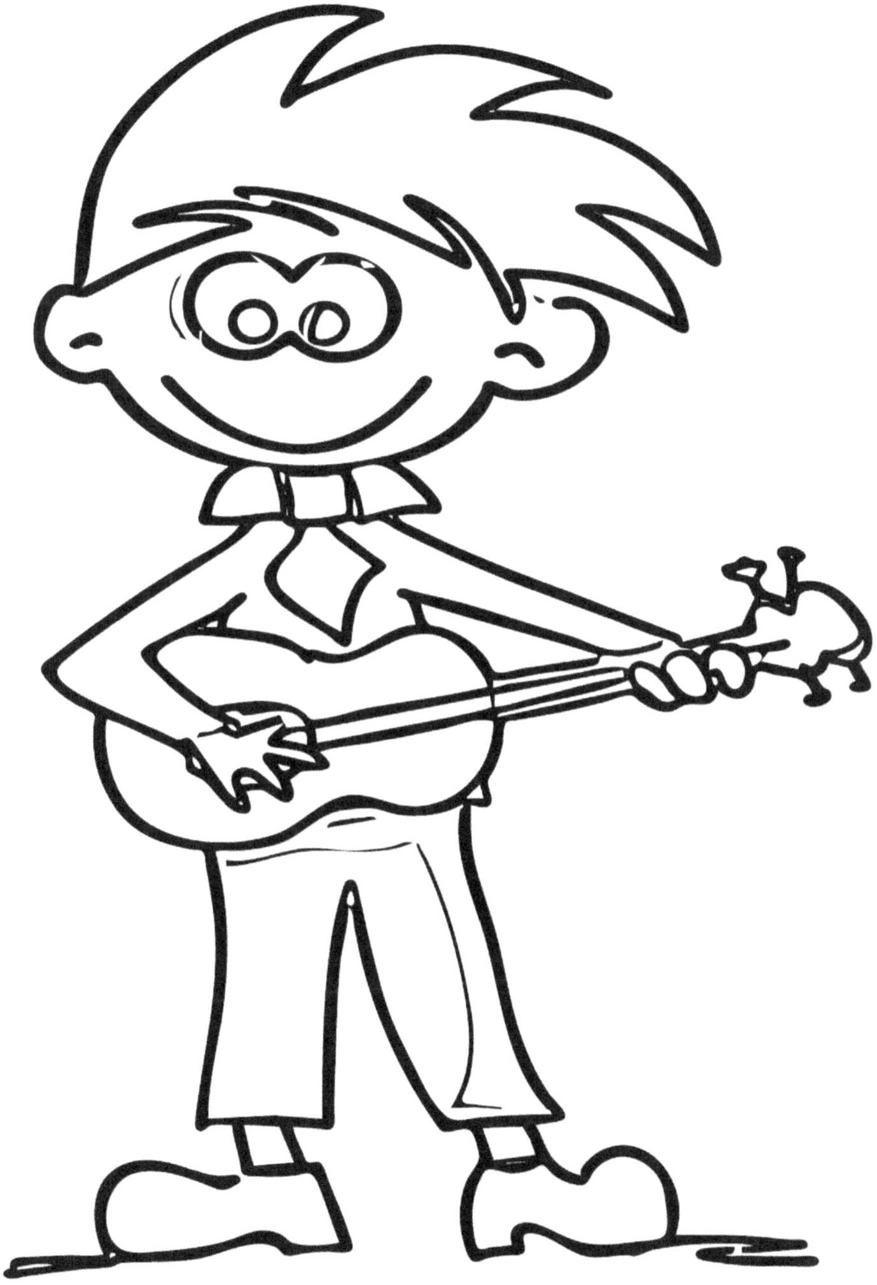

www.ingramcontent.com/pod-product-compliance
Lightning Source LLC
Chambersburg PA
CBHW081550170526
45166CB00009B/2644
*9781519298416*